secrets of **sexual**
body **language**

secrets of sexual
body language

Martin Lloyd-Elliott

Amorata Press

Published in 2006 in the United States by
Amorata Press, an imprint of Ulysses Press
P.O. Box 3440
Berkeley, CA 94703
www.amoratapress.com

First published in the United Kingdom by Hamlyn,
an imprint of Octopus Publishing Group

Library of Congress Control Number 2005908372
ISBN 1-56975-524-8

Cover Design: Sarah Levin
U.S. Proofreader: Lily Chou

Printed and bound in China
10 9 8 7 6 5 4 3 2 1

Distributed by Publishers Group West

Note The contents of this book are based on personal
observations of human interaction and on numerous
scientific research projects. Despite the obvious existence
of distinct behavioural patterns and courtship rituals it
should be noted that all human beings are individuals
and that every transpersonal interaction is a unique event
requiring thoughtful consideration and the application of
courtesy and common sense.

Contents

Introduction	6
Personal space	14
Tell-tale signs	32
First impressions	46
The eyes	62
The mouth	82
Body talk	100
Using all the senses	130
The whole picture	142
Bibliography	156
Index	158
Acknowledgments	160

Introduction

I am a psychologist who works as a psychotherapist.

The standard stranger's response to discovering what I do for a living is, all too often, to assume I am going to analyze their every word, to presume that I can read their body language and their mind and to accuse me of intending to turn this secret knowledge to my own advantage. This response typifies a popular misconception of psychology. Luckily, with the rapid growth in the study of psychology in higher education, more people now realize that the science of mental life touches a vast array of different aspects of human behavior, and that psychologists work in areas as diverse as business, hospitals, schools, advertising, the media, police and government. But one thread that links most psychologists' work is an awareness of the central importance of relationships between people. Relationships rely on good communication. This book is about a crucial aspect of human communication.

Humans and sex

We humans are sexual beings and sex is a principal motivator in our lives. Beyond the short-term gratification of great sex lies the much greater and universally shared longing for a meaningful relationship and love. How we set about searching for another person to love and be loved by often occupies a large amount of our thinking time (awake, day-dreaming and asleep). In the process of this search, misunderstandings occur usually because we have failed to comprehend or perhaps even think about the non-verbal signals that we are sending out to others and receiving back from them. It is possible to change – but you may need to do some uncomfortable self-searching in order to increase your self-awareness, and ultimately improve your self-confidence.

Happiness, joy and laughter are the most attractive qualities we can exhibit.

Non-verbal communication

We humans are curious beings. We like looking at each other. The body speaks. Every person scans tens if not hundreds of people every day, either in life or on a television or computer screen. The workings of our visual cortex are dominant among the sensory functions. We assess each other constantly. Like it or not, we categorize, compare, judge, assume and project, and all that takes place in a few seconds. As soon as we find ourselves in a public space, we search the environment, consciously or unconsciously looking for a face we recognize, seeking out interesting-looking people or perhaps for someone we like. How much notice you take of this function will vary according to your individual circumstances. If you are single and feeling horny, your attention will be more focused on identifying potential mates than if you are in love and committed to monogamy.

Your interest in those around you will also be affected by many other factors including your physical health (having sex while you're feeling ill is not much fun), your mental health (being depressed and aroused are relatively incompatible) and, if you are female and fertile, the day you have reached in your menstrual cycle.

These two people are mirroring each other's posture and movements – note the position of their arms and hands – indicating mutual attraction and a desire for synchrony.

And while your conscious mind is wondering if what you have read applies to you, the extraordinary thing we call the unconscious is exercising its influence and control over your sexual reactions to everyone around you, including:

- Desire – the whiff of a delectable perfume
- Repulsion – at a pair of obviously fake breasts the size of watermelons and lip implants like bee stings
- Arousal – a distant memory of a first love rekindled by the shape of the back of the head of someone sitting in front of you
- Lack of interest – a curious invisibility that excludes those who fall outside our prerequisites for sexual response.

Some of these influences may be instinctive, genetic or beyond reason (perky breasts cheer up almost all men instantly, while tall, athletic, square-jawed, ruggedly beautiful men make womens' hearts beat faster). Other influences may be cultural (such as thin androgynous waifs as icons of beauty in Western advertising). Yet others are directly related to our own unique story (we seem curiously drawn to people who look like us or like one of our parents).

Conscious and unconscious forces operate in all areas of our lives and nowhere more so than in our sexual encounters. What images are conjured in your visual imagination when you contemplate sexual attraction? Do you see the object of your sexual desire, your fantasy lover, your ideal partner, or do you see other people being lustful?

So, just what is this thing we call sexual attraction – urgent, compelling, intoxicating, salivating, carnal and shortlived? Is it possible for anyone to maintain a state of authentic desire for long? Or does it last only as long as the object of desire remains just out of reach? Perhaps sexual attraction is the state we reach when not getting what we want most?

Bars provide endless opportunities to spot signals of attraction. There are six separate positive gestures among the people in this group.

Can women experience sexual desire as intensely as men? Yes, of course they can, they just don't act on the impulse with as much enthusiasm or regularity as men. In 1989 psychologists carried out a study in which an attractive female stranger approached men on a university campus and suggested they go to bed. Some 75 percent of the men responded positively. In contrast, when a similar approach was made to women by a male stranger, none of the women agreed.

Men often ask me what they can do differently to be more successful in attracting women. I tell them the obvious stuff first: pay attention to your personal hygiene; check your breath; be gallant; try listening for a change instead of talking; stay focused and stop looking over her shoulder for another possibility; avoid drooling and don't stare at her cleavage; stay sober. This list is embarrassingly obvious yet it is perhaps more alarming that so many men seem to be unaware of even these simple rules. Some of these rules may also apply to women, but mostly, women find it significantly easier to attract a mate than men do.

However, these rules are not the advanced body-language skills of sexual attraction. This book will detail every aspect of the art of sexual body language that men, and to some extent, women, could do with revising.

Men are often guilty of "wandering eye" syndrome, which women find insulting and unattractive.

What women find most attractive about men are things like competence. If you are an expert at almost anything you will feel more confident and have a sense of who you are. This will show in every aspect of your body language, from the way you walk to the way you look at a woman. And women want men with soul, with passion, with vitality, with a twinkle in their eyes, with the promise of an intense, ecstatic life. When men have found a mission, show courage, conviction and competence, they feel fully alive and this connects them to their potency. They feel sexy, and if they feel sexy they will be sexy.

So perhaps sexual attraction can take on other less shadowy meanings for us and include playfulness, vigor, intensity, vitality and ecstatic pleasure.

Why the bias towards men, you might be thinking? Well, women are simply better at sensing and responding to non-verbal cues. If I presume to consider where women might change their body language, it is either related to their concerns over excessive male attention, usually triggered by their highly flirtatious unconscious behavior; or their worries about failing to attract men, which usually relates to a mismatch between their internal sexual interest and their external concerns to appear chaste because they believe this is more likely to lead to love.

A twinkle in the eye, a confident touch and a warm smile are an irresistible combination.

Evolutionary biologists and anthropologists have traditionally argued that sexual attraction is the fuse of life. It is the trigger for initiating mating behavior. We are genetically programmed to reproduce our genes. So that's it then. We are all operating under Darwin's urge – women should only feel lustful towards tall hairy men built like Greek gods. This idea points us towards one of many paradoxes – woman's evolutionary programming should tell them to have sex with men who demonstrate good health and strong male characteristics, but they also need men who will stick around and help protect the children. As a consequence what is appealing to women is as varied as the male population. Actually, we humans can have sex whenever we like, irrespective of the likelihood of producing children. Our bodies are designed for sexual pleasure.

It is a misconception that men initiate sexual encounters. Two-thirds of all flirtatious encounters are initiated by women. Researchers have called this behavior "female proceptivity." In our chimpanzee relatives, this proceptivity is gloriously transparent – female chimps actively solicit sex with males, going as far as pulling a resting male to his feet and insisting on copulation. The human equivalent, to men's relief or disappointment, depending on your point of view, is deceptively concealed and deliciously cunning. In fact, human female solicitation is done so subtly that most men think they are initiating rather than responding. Research published in 2003 suggests that a woman bombards a man with a variety of flirtatious signals designed to encourage him to reveal his true nature so that she can then make a more informed choice of mate.

So is sexual attraction just lust? Of course it isn't. The most important sexual organ in the body is the brain, and the brain influences our sexual behavior and feelings in a myriad of different ways. Our non-verbal communication is vital because at first it is all a potential mate has to go on. The way we look and the way we are looked at are central to sexual triggers.

Confidence, clear communication and passion are all highly attractive qualities.

Self-beautification and preening are essential preparation rituals for sexual attraction.

Perhaps we are in danger of becoming obsessed with our looks and the looks of those we presume to desire. In doing so we ignore a simple truth. The way we appear is a consequence of the way we feel inside. When a woman says, "I was very attracted by the way he looked," what she often means is, "I liked the look in his eyes when he looked at me." Our body language reveals our inner truths. Many books on body language encourage people to change their external behavior. "No," I say, "rather, review and change your internals. Question yourself. Get to know yourself. Become self-aware. Identify your truths."

If you want to be more successful in the whole business of reading the body language of sexual attraction – become conscious of your own behavior. Play to your strengths: be realistic, mindful, sensitive and attentive to detail. Become expert, practice and develop empathy.

In writing a popular psychology book, my aim is that you will be inspired to read around the subject, so that psychology plays a greater part in your life. Used well, a knowledge of psychology can enhance your life and that of those around you. It can relieve distress and anxiety and empower you to become a more sensitive, confident and successful person in your relationships.

It will not give you any magic powers – you don't need magic since you already have at your disposal a fabulous array of senses, each one of which you are probably using at half capacity or less. Sight, taste, touch, hearing and smell, and then, of course, your sixth sense – radar, intuition, gut reaction, call it what you will – all of these have a great role to play in building your talent when it comes to the art of seduction without words.

The first and most important secret in the success of understanding sexual body language is ruthless honesty. Honesty and truth to yourself and to other people is the key to happiness. It is pointless pretending to be something or someone that you are not in order to seduce someone because, if it succeeds, the relationship is based on a false premise and ultimately it will fail.

In an age where the risk of infection from sexually transmitted diseases must force us to exercise great caution before entering fully blown sexual encounters, and at a time when so many relationships end in great sadness, recrimination and even financial ruin, the sensitive application of some of the observations in this text will, I hope, help people to be more self-aware and sensitive to the amazingly vital, tantalizing world of non-verbal communication, particularly as it applies to the central motivators of our existence – love and sex.

Be soulful. Be passionate. Be animated. Act from a place of integrity. People find authenticity very sexy. Be joyful and vital. Be fit. Work on your health. Learn to inhabit your body well. Do Pilates. Learn how to move to rhythm – take dance lessons. Learn to breathe properly and relax. Do yoga. But most of all, be loving and be joyful. Loving life and living joyfully permeates every part of your being and will make your body language irresistible.

If you follow your bliss, bliss will seek you out.

Authentic attraction is revealed by intense focus and synchrony of movement and mood.

Personal space

As human beings, we are very affected by our surroundings. All of our senses make us good at monitoring events in the environment, from sensing vibrations in the ground beneath our feet to developing a pre-thunderstorm headache even before black clouds gather overhead. Our senses are the key to the survival of our species. We can detect potentially harmful objects approaching us at speed, and take preventative action. We can smell when food has gone bad and can detect the subtlest changes in body odor. We all sense when someone out of our line of vision is staring at us and can be aware of the close proximity of another person even when there is no physical contact. Everyone has the ability to sense another person's vibes or guess at their moods. Some people even claim to be able to see the color of individuals' auras – energy fields that exist around all of us.

Attitudes towards personal space

The study of distance between people during communication is called proxemics. A working understanding of proxemics is a must if you want to improve your non-verbal sexual communication skills.

What is your attitude towards your personal space? This will depend on the culture of your original family. Culture is like water to a fish – we are immersed in it. Some families are touchy-feely and happily squeeze together on one sofa to watch television. Others are remote and awkward, never hugging or cuddling. Our core reactions to intimacy are laid down like blueprints in childhood. Are you an only child? If you are, then you are probably more selfish with your space than someone who has had to share with siblings. You may still guard your personal space jealously and letting potential mates close in may be something you will need to work on.

Extrovert or introvert?

Are you an extrovert or introvert? Extroverts tend to allow people to come physically closer to them without experiencing any discomfort. Shy introverts usually want to hold other people at arm's length, at the very least, and ideally to keep people far enough away from them to be able to keep a watchful eye on the whole person. Extroverts tend to seek out the company of others and enjoy the close proximity that companionship often brings; their inclination is to move in closer. If an extrovert is attracted to an introvert, an absurd unconscious dance can follow – every time the extrovert closes in on the introvert's space, the latter will take a step backwards. The extrovert may interpret this as a "come-on" and take another step closer, the introvert then retreats further, and so on.

Each person has an invisible bubble of personal space surrounding them. In social settings we are acutely aware of invasions of that space by others and often respond to advances with subtle defense postures like crossing our arms in front of us.

How tactile are you?

Are you someone who hugs close friends and relatives or was it normal in your family not to touch your parents?

Do you find touch easy or stressful? Do you like giving and receiving massages, or do you jump if anyone touches you? Do you dread the closeness of a first slow dance or do you try to turn a fast dance into a slow one if given the chance? How sensitive are you to the touch of others? If you are standing on a crowded train squeezed up against four or five other people, are you very conscious of which bits are touching or are you oblivious to the physical contact? Your level of tactile tolerance or enjoyment affects how aroused you become when others move into close proximity with you.

1 Beyond arm's length we feel comfortable with strangers. Once eye contact is made we are aware of the distance. His torso is half-facing her, suggesting he is non-threatening. She can take in his whole "picture" and assess her next move.

2 She has moved into his personal space, turning her head to one side in acknowledgement of his invitation to approach. She lifts her right shoulder seductively and he moves his body so that his eyes are on a level with hers.

3 She lets him move into her intimate space zone. Close proximity leads to physiological arousal. Eye contact combined with hand touches creates an electric atmosphere charged with sexual tension.

Social, personal and intimate space

Your brain has a choice of emotional responses to metabolic arousal.
Whether you experience fear, anger or pleasure when in a crowded situation
is influenced by the following:

- The circumstances of the interaction
- The sex of the people crowding you
- Your age
- Your personality
- Where you live and the culture in which you grew up
- How intimate your relationship is with the other person.

The people we welcome into our intimate space are those with whom we
have close bonds. It requires a high degree of trust to let anyone close enough
to touch any part of our body with any part of theirs. City-dwellers are generally
better at sharing their physical space than people who live in the country:
a country person will perceive a city dweller's automatic urge to stand close
during conversation as rude or threatening. Be sensitive to people's need for
personal space. If they step back when you approach it does not automatically
mean they are not attracted to you; they just need more space to feel
comfortable. It is vital that a person you are attracted to feels comfortable in
any exchange, otherwise their need to stick to their own rules for personal
space will override any attraction they might feel.

Power play

**Avoid dominance and power plays. Men often exploit their
height advantage to imply power or status. While tall and
high-status men may be rated as attractive, a bad impression
is created if you imply a need to dominate and control. It is
inadvisable to enter another's personal space zone from a
position of height.**

If a man is sitting at a desk he will unconsciously perceive it as attacking
or challenging if a woman moves into his space and remains standing
up. If a woman is on the telephone and a man encroaches on her territory
by, for example, putting a briefcase, a cup of coffee or a file on her desk,
this will not be conducive to any feelings of attraction. The same can be
said if he leans over her desk or sits on it. However, if the man indicates
with his hands or facial expression that he would like to sit on her desk
and permission is granted with a nod and a smile, covert or overt feelings
of attraction will be in the air. When a woman has a dominant position,
power plays are seen as disarming by the fragile male ego.

Sex and cultural differences

The sex of the person moving into our personal space is crucial to our response. Men tend to assume that when a woman moves into their intimate space she is making a sexual move towards them.

Women tolerate physical invasion of their space by other women to a much higher degree than they accept it from men. In contrast, men perceive an approach from another man as highly threatening and competitive or sexual. When a man moves into another man's personal space uninvited, the latter's state of metabolic arousal will be one of fear or anger. When a man moves into a woman's space uninvited, in the absence of any positive or friendly non-verbal cues, she will feel threatened. If a woman moves into a man's space, he will see it as a high-scoring, non-verbal sexual advance. As the saying goes, "If you stand close enough to a man for him to kiss you, he'll probably try."

Using your knowledge of proxemics, you can balance how you position yourself in relation to a potential mate's personal space without causing any discomfort. Becoming "close" to someone emotionally also happens literally. This is best achieved through an unspoken mutual agreement that you overlap and then merge your spaces.

A Swedish woman who moved to Australia was regarded with hostility as a flirt and potential marriage breaker by local women. Compared with the norm in Sweden, Australian women stand 7 inches further away from men with whom they are socializing and not flirting.

Global differences

Cultural differences and national characteristics are significant when it comes to personal space.

How much space people require in order to feel comfortable relates directly to how much they touch each other, non-sexually, during normal conversation. People from Spain, Portugal, Italy and Greece all touch quite a lot, so they stand within easy touching distance when with friends. People from Latin America and the Middle East tend to touch even more and stand very close during both verbal and non-verbal exchanges. On the other hand, North Americans, Britons, most Northern Europeans and Australians generally react very negatively if you come too close. You should always take the cultural background of people into consideration. The saying, "When in Rome, do as the Romans do," is an important one to bear in mind.

Invading personal space

How do you speed up the merging of two people's intimate spaces? The secret is to set up a situation where it becomes possible to offer or receive an invitation to come closer, or where invasion appears to be in response to an invitation, even if none has actually been offered.

Men: Avoid sitting or standing immediately alongside a woman, at least to start with. Women feel most at ease if a man approaches them from the front, not from behind or the side. Once contact is established they feel most comfortable if the man then moves to one side to continue the interaction. You should also avoid sitting or standing alongside a woman you are interested in and attracted to. It is much easier to flirt across a dinner table and the ideal position is diagonally opposite each other.

Women: Don't approach men full face; they find this potentially threatening and challenging. Approach a man from the side and then slowly move around to face him if you wish to turn the romantic heat up.

Avoid dominance and power plays, and never enter someone's close personal space from a position of height. Men often exploit their extra height advantage to convey power or status. While tall and high-status men may generally be rated as being more attractive, using this might imply a need to dominate and control and is very off-putting. If a man is sitting at a desk, he will see a woman moving into his space standing up as attacking or challenging.

Her signals of attraction include direct eye contact, her leg-cross and knee-point towards him, her smile, her hand on her thigh and the fact that she has turned her chair so her torso faces him directly. He signals his interest in her by lowering himself so that their eyes meet on a similar level. His open body posture, palm display and hand-point are further clues, and his invasion of her personal territory is done in such a way that it seems neither aggressive nor domineering.

Territory

Every object within a work space carries a message – the open or closed door, the pictures, the design of chair, the size of desk, chaotic piles of paper, awards in fancy frames. The way we arrange our space says much about status, power, attraction and availability. In many workplaces people mark their territory and guard it jealously.

Men are generally more competitive about their space than women. Men tend to regard all invasions of their territory, however friendly, as potential threats. Women are generally much more tolerant of sharing their space with others, and especially with other women. Men like to mark out their territory, keeping the boundaries clear by the equivalent of spraying their scent in every corner. This primitive urge is part of the instinct to create a space within which the man feels dominant and into which he wants to attract females.

In a social setting, if the person into whose space you wish to be invited is sitting down, lower your eye level to meet theirs. The eyes and mouth are central to non-verbal sexual signals (see pages 62–99). Therefore, one of your first considerations should be how best you can align your eyes with theirs.

Her stiff neck and awkward posture show her discomfort. Her arm is crossed in front of her, protecting her from his dominant display and more threatening invasion of her intimate personal space zone. His palm down on her desk top, the angle of his leaning torso, his stare and smirky expression are all more aggressive than his previous position, but may still be regarded as sexy.

Open gestures and smiles

Open body gestures and welcoming smiles are great ways to attract a person into our own personal space – simply by making it inviting.

Use open body gestures to create open territory lines into which someone will be attracted to move. In principle it means we should create the illusion of being a rewarding door at the end of a triangle-shaped corridor towards which people will automatically be drawn. We want people to feel that the door at the end of the corridor is inviting, tempting, exciting, maybe even a little dangerous, arousing and attractive. Simultaneously we can give out warm rays of sunlight into which people wish to step. Being in the rays makes them feel good, and in feeling good they are more attracted to the source of the feeling. This human sunlight takes the form of big, sincere and generous smiles, plenty of open gestures, inviting body postures, and a quieter rather than louder voice.

If you decide to invade someone's personal space you must override their fear or anger responses by giving them a high dose of positive non-verbal messages. You should move towards them slowly and gently, exchanging brief bursts of eye contact interspersed with lowered eyes, all the time punctuated with a symmetrical smile and small nodding and encouraging movements of the head every five seconds or so. Meanwhile, keep your hands open and expressive and your attitude light and easy rather than intense.

When you speak, ask questions, listen to their answers, be positive, flattering, warm and complimentary about them, their tastes, their home – whatever your compliment, they must know your words are really meant for them. Smiles elicit smiles. If you can get someone to open up with a smile, their body language and unconscious feelings will soon follow. When we smile, our mood immediately lifts. With an elevated mood comes relaxation and pleasure.

Her animated conversation, their open gestures, his active listening and their obvious mutual attraction lead to touching, teasing and a pillow fight. When flirting and playfulness get physical, the accompanying metabolic arousal often leads to sexual encounters.

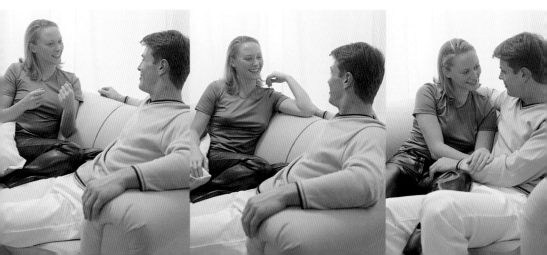

1 He adopts the classic cowboy stance, hands in pockets, pointing towards his crotch. She mirrors a similar position. They hold each other's gaze, smiling and open-bodied.

2 She moves her left foot close to his right foot, nearly touching him. Her hand position is open, her arms back slightly, pushing her breasts towards him. His open palm facing upwards is another friendly inviting gesture.

Side-on and full-face approaches

Picking the right way to approach someone in social situations is just as important as in the workplace.

Lovers often speak very quietly to each other. It is part of the sexual exchange that takes place within the merged intimate spaces. If we speak clearly but quietly people move closer to us in order to hear us properly. This is a wonderful way of inviting someone to come close.

The secret to success is to arrange yourself to optimum intimate effect in relation to another's space without causing discomfort. By its very nature, increased intimacy is constrained or enhanced by two people's relative proximity. Becoming "close" to someone emotionally is enacted literally. This is best achieved through an unspoken mutual agreement that you overlap and then merge your touching space zones.

How does one increase the speed with which the merging of intimate zones occurs? Unfortunately our culture has specific rules about invading or defending personal space and it can be uncomfortable to feel invaded or to encroach too far. The secret is to avoid invasion at all. Instead, set up a situation where it becomes possible to offer or receive an open invitation to come closer to someone, or where encroaching appears to be in response to an invitation, even if none has been offered.

Moving into the intimate zone

For someone to invite you into their personal space and, subsequently, their intimate zone, they must be feeling good about themselves and you.

Other people's lives are full of influences over which we have no control. If you are attracted to someone who is obviously not feeling good, do not try to encroach on their intimate space without a specific invitation. Offering someone the physical comfort or the reassurance of an arm or a shoulder to cry on may be the first intimate contact you establish, but do not take it for granted that your offer will be accepted.

Even simple exchanges between two people can lead one of them to open up. Once they let down their barriers, the mood may change and greater intimacy may be welcomed – for example, by handing someone with their arms tightly crossed a drink, you cause them to lower their defenses as they reach out to accept the glass. To be invited to enter another person's intimate space is a privilege and a precious gift. It should be accepted graciously and acknowledged gently and sensitively.

Invading space with objects

People often use an object to invade another person's space. Pens, cutlery, wine glasses, cigarettes, candles or whatever can be slid across table tops as if they were chess pieces being sent into battle or ambassadors on a mission to represent our hearts' desires.

If you are having dinner and you slide a piece of cutlery over the halfway mark of the table and into the other person's space, their reaction will be telling. If they hold on to the object or keep touching it, then they are attracted to you. If they push your object back to your side of the table, this is an indication that you should back off and accept that romance may not be in the air, or at least take the hint that you are rushing things and they want you to slow down. Bear in mind that just because someone does not immediately respond to your maneuver, does not necessarily mean that they aren't attracted to you or never will be.

Remember that the majority of non-verbal behaviors take place without our conscious awareness. Commenting aloud on observed unconscious reactions can be insulting, unsettling and a turn-off. The expert application of body-language awareness should be undetectable.

He is breaching the territorial mid-line on the table, taking possession of all the space with his arms. She is fondling the phallic stem of her glass, unconsciously holding his gaze, her leg pushing forward between his, all of which suggest that she is accepting and perhaps even enjoying his dominance.

Leaving a bit of ourselves behind

Sometimes we leave things behind in people's personal space by "accident": a pair of glasses, a pen on a co-worker's desk or an umbrella propped behind a door; they are all ways of saying that we do not want to leave, and of providing a good excuse to return another day. This may happen without our being consciously aware of it.

Invading space with our bodies

People invade the personal space of others with various parts of their bodies. Our hands are our most obvious non-verbal communicators.

Hands make gestures to represent actual words, to symbolize acts, and to illustrate, emphasize and enliven our verbal conversation. We also use our hands to move into other people's space and we often have ample opportunity to place our hands where they can be touched by another person – either intentionally or not. From the formal non-threatening handshake to the intimate stroke of a neck or face, the hands are used to indicate interest in another person. The way in which we use our hands, arms and legs will indicate the intent that lies behind the gesture.

Other forms of space invasion

Sometimes pets provide the link that brings people into each other's space.

For example, a beautiful and friendly dog on a long leash has been used many a time to reel in an attractive man or woman like a big fish on a hook. We also use inanimate objects to represent ourselves in other people's space. We give mementoes, letters, flowers and gifts, all of which are symbolic of our actual selves. We are in another's intimate space by proxy, as it were. This is why clothes are so intimate; when a woman lends a man her scarf and he wraps it around his neck, then symbolically she is in some way intimately connected with him.

Flirting in traffic

For several generations men had a virtual monopoly on the car as bait for women. These days more women are expressing status, power, wealth, excitement and personality through their choice of car.

Cars can be very sexy. Most men and many women regard cars as crucial indicators of status – we arrange cars into hierarchies of desirability much the way we do each other. Their design, color, rarity, cost and power all get transferred from metal to flesh.

Driving, especially in the age of endless traffic jams, provides opportunities for exploring sexual body language. Dedicated flirts take every opportunity to flash eyebrows, share a smile, to wink at or catch the eye of other attractive drivers. People have reported "falling in love" with another's eyes, by merely

Making eye contact in another driver's rear-view mirror is surprisingly easy. Traffic lights provide endless possibilities for flirting practice.

glancing in their rear-view mirror. Few encounters between drivers develop, but their value for practicing flirting should not be missed.

As an extension of our personal space our cars, reveal a lot about our personality and our lifestyle – a grubby interior full of trash is a world away from a sparkling clean pride and joy; a 1960s Austin Healey makes a style statement quite removed from that made by a flashy new Ferrari.

And the way we actually drive also sends clear signals to the opposite sex. How we handle the car gives clues as to how we will be in bed: clumsy, confident, aggressive, smooth, selfish, nervous, arrogant, over-eager, running the lights… and this is true for both men and women. However, all men greatly overestimate their driving skills. Young men, usually trying to improve their sense of potency, are the most reckless and stupid of all drivers. They reveal more about their sexual competence than they know.

Convertibles make flirting in traffic much easier. Being open to the elements creates the illusion of being more "natural" and, because of not being boxed in, more available, too.

Tell-tale signs

No matter what we may be saying verbally, or implying with meaningful silences, our bodies carry on a continual dialogue with the outside world. Our brains are constantly busy, and as a consequence we can only allocate a percentage of mental energy to monitoring our own non-verbal signals. We tend to concentrate on controlling our faces because the face is the most important part of the body involved in non-verbal communication. The vast majority of these processes are unconscious.

Facial expressions and other leakage

We can read a great deal about the moods of people around us just by observing their unconscious facial expressions and body language, without them having to say a word.

Our face frames our eyes and mouth, perhaps the two most important features in non-verbal signalling. While we can control our facial expressions to disguise our feelings to a large extent, we are less skilled at monitoring and containing our body movements and reflexes. When we attempt to control such movements, our body still sends out non-verbal messages. Psychologists call these tics and twitches "non-verbal leakage." Our hands, fingers and feet are especially good giveaways. If we stop our fingers from drumming, our feet start tapping instead; if we concentrate on keeping our feet still, then perhaps a shoulder or elbow will twitch. Our hands, arms, feet and legs can also betray our attraction to someone (see pages 100–129).

1 The symmetry of a genuine smile is unmistakable. The muscles around the mouth and eyes are relaxed. The feeling portrayed is easily identified and the viewer can experience a similar mood by copying the expression.

2 Many facial expressions are more subtle and require detailed scrutiny. Sometimes we witness ambiguous "mixed" signals, or display incongruity, for example, when the eyes show alert interest but the mouth shows sadness.

Out of sight, out of mind. Under pressure, feet "leak" information about our true level of arousal, tapping and drawing circles in the air without our realizing it.

Due to the complex muscles of the face, we are capable of making thousands of different expressions. Many of the muscle movements are tiny and can only be identified using slow-motion film, but our brains are so fine-tuned to communication that our unconscious will detect the meaning of the movements even if our conscious does not

Pointing

We use subtle pointing in two different ways: to indicate our interest in another person, and to draw attention to ourselves.

When we are attracted to someone we will often point towards them – not obviously, with a finger, but quietly and seductively, with our eyes, our hands and arms, our legs, feet and toes. It is as though we indicate our sexual interest in someone by pointing at them to pick them out in a crowd.

We also point with our hands at what we consider our own best sexual assets, as well as at the parts of our body that are most significant for a particular non-verbal communication, for example our eyes and mouth.

If you learn to read pointing, not only can you recognize when someone is showing an interest in you, but you can also respond subtly to indicate a mutual interest or make sure that they notice your best points!

Many exchanges early on in romantic encounters are very subtle. The accidental hand touch is typical. Often momentary, the fingers briefly brush against each other, apparently innocently but loaded with intention.

Context

Don't forget to take into account where you are and the circumstances you find yourself in.

It may seem obvious but it's amazing how many people are unaware of sending inappropriate signals in the wrong setting; for example, perhaps using flirty non-verbal sexual signals at work to "persuade" someone to do something they want, then wondering what's hit them when the totally predictable, sometimes embarrassing response occurs.

Environmental factors, particularly temperature, can affect our body language, for example. It may simply be that the person you are interested in has adopted an apparently defensive arm-crossed stance because they're freezing cold rather than uninterested! Similarly, at formal events, where people are required to adopt stiff postures, relaxed interpersonal communication will be difficult. It's also very difficult to be relaxed in tight or very elaborate clothes that restrict physical movement.

His left foot, hands, head and body are all pointing towards his date. Her right foot points directly at him, probably without her realizing, confirming her attraction to him. Men who focus all their attention on the woman they are with are so much sexier than the more usual "wandering eye" man.

Peek-a-boo

This is a very simple game that we play as infants and continue to play in a variety of forms in our adult lives, particularly during the process of seduction.

We play peek-a-boo, hiding behind newspapers or menus and allowing short, tantalizing glimpses of our eyes. We also use our clothes to play peek-a-boo: flashing various bits of our flesh at each other through gaps and tears in our clothes, tapping into those early, intensely joyful memories of peek-a-boo when it was one of the few games we were able to play.

Peek-a-boo imposes the excitement of anticipation. The longer the eyes are concealed, the greater the tension and the more pleasurable the relief when concealment is removed to reveal smiling eyes. The effect is similar to the interruption of the sun's warm rays by a passing cloud. The renewed pleasure of the sunlight (and the gaze) is somehow increased by it having been temporarily denied us.

This man is using his menu to play peek-a-boo with a woman at a nearby table. He could just as easily use a cup or glass to interrupt their line of vision to play his game. Peering around a menu in this way, establishing eye contact and then disappearing again can induce a feeling of merriment in both participants that is disproportionate to the actual event.

Blocking

Blocking is a strong signal used by couples who don't want to be interrupted as a means of warding off potential rivals and as a means of making it clear that they're not interested.

The aim of blocking is to use your body to establish boundaries around the two of you to create a private and safe haven, but not so close as to make the other person uncomfortable. Established lovers do this obviously with their arms interlocking or with an intense mutual gaze from which the rest of the world feels excluded, and within which the lovers are oblivious, entranced by each other's eyes.

Blocking is also a useful skill for sending "I'm not interested" messages without having the embarrassment of needing to spell it out in words. By building a wall with non-verbal blocks around us we can protect ourselves, comfort ourselves and warn others off; our arms, legs, shoulders and body position can all be employed as a means of saying "no thanks."

Pushing between the couple already at the bar may appear innocent, but by placing herself in the middle, she immediately blocks the seated woman and gives him no choice but to take immediate note of her presence.

Echoing and mirroring

You don't have to mirror movements exactly: if she's holding on to the stem of her wine glass, wait for a bit and then hold the top of the glass or the base. If you keep copying her exactly, it will disturb her.

When we are attracted to someone else it is usually for one of two main reasons: either we sense a similarity between us or we anticipate that we will complement each other. During the early stages of a romantic encounter, we automatically highlight the things we have in common. This expresses itself in two forms: postural echoes and mirroring behavior.

Echoing

Postural echoing is when one person takes up a particular body posture and the other follows, adopting a similar or even identical posture between 5 and 50 seconds later. If someone echoes your posture, they are comfortable in your company and probably attracted to you. Check how interested they are by changing your position and see if they follow you. The more they follow you the more interested they are.

If you want to let them know you are interested, send them a strong signal by following their movements. The skill lies in echoing the other person's posture without copying them exactly. You need to capture the spirit of the position rather than the letter. By doing this you are moving towards mirroring.

Easy does it!

If they keep changing position as soon as you echo their new posture, they may be sending you a "not interested" message or perhaps saying, "You're going too fast, slow it down a bit, please." In any case, back off both physically and non-verbally. Turn down the heat a bit.

Never judge a book by its cover. Non-verbal communication can be very ambiguous. Most people's judgements of others' thoughts and feelings are based on insufficient information. Clarification gained by checking for additional body signals always triumphs over unreliable assumptions.

Mirroring

As you become attracted to someone, you begin to tune into their wavelength and, if the feelings are mutual, they tune into yours.

Some couples report that after only a short time together they seem to be able to think and move in synchrony. It is as if they have become one person, reaching for their drinks or folding their arms simultaneously, leaning forwards or back like choreographed dancers. This makes both individuals feel potent, affirmed, recognized, wanted, attractive, warm and desirable.

Research has shown that people who are deeply in love or close friends who have known each other a long time automatically develop this ability to tune in to the smallest movement. We use similar hand gestures, take up matching body torso postures, and tilt our heads to the same angle, helping to keep our eyes aligned.

Full mirroring versus half mirroring

If your partner has their right elbow on a table at which you are sitting face to face, you can either put your left elbow on the table to match your partner's right elbow (full mirroring) or you can put your right elbow on the table (half mirroring).

When sitting opposite each other eating a meal, you can half mirror by lifting your fork to your mouth at the same time as each other, both using the same hand. If you are sitting side by side at a bar, a full mirroring movement is a more powerful non-verbal sexual signal.

Mirroring body positions and space zones

Mirroring is a powerful affirmation of sexual interest, indicating that you are operating on the same wavelength.

1 Her reaction to his initial approach is disdain, her expression hostile and arm defensive. He has the advantage of being below her, which reduces the threat of his intention. He smiles and jokes and slowly breaks down her defenses.

2 He adopts exactly the same body posture as her, mirroring her to make her feel in synchrony with him. His right shoulder angles his torso around to face her. He tilts his head slightly to one side to indicate that he is listening carefully to her. Although her torso still faces the pool, she smiles at him over her shoulder, which is extremely flirtatious.

3 Some time later she rearranges her body position into a much more relaxed and intimate stance. Her head leaning towards him, her obvious acceptance of his close proximity and the way in which her knees are drawn up, sending an unconscious sexual signal by mimicking breasts, all suggest that strong mutual attraction exists between them.

Putting it into practice

The idea is to speed up the process of getting closer to someone by deliberately increasing the amount and degree of echo and mirroring.

The first rule is: don't play "copy cat" – you will be quickly figured out by the other person. Secondly, if the other person is genuinely interested, some mirroring will already be happening. Increased echoing and mirroring has the effect of exaggerating the positive feelings of attraction that may already be developing between you.

Sometimes you may discover yourself mirroring someone to whom you are not sure of feeling attracted. An increased sense of self-awareness is one of the most valuable skills you can develop when you are learning to enhance your own non-verbal communication skills. If you can manage to ignore all the different thoughts that are whirling around in your head and focus your concentration on what your own body language is telling you, you will find yourself increasingly attracted towards people who are also attracted to you.

The way to become an expert in all these different skills is through application and practice. The purpose of this book is to help you accomplish a movement of non-verbal translation from an unconscious to a conscious level. Once you become conscious of your own and other people's pointing, blocking, context, posture, echoing and mirroring, new worlds of communication open up to you.

Practice makes perfect. Look at the world around you: watch television with the sound turned down. Study your favorite actors and analyze their body language. What is there that you like so much? What are their most sensuous movements? Can you replicate them?

Study people everywhere. Notice how they flirt when they laugh, flick their hair or display their necks by tilting their heads back. The street is your very own public university, full of information. The players in this wonderful game are all around you, at work, on the train and in your local café.

First impressions

You walk into a crowded party thronged with people dancing, drinking or chatting. Everyone will notice you.

How long they look at you and the major decisions they make about you will depend almost entirely on your non-verbal signals. We form our main impressions about people within the first few seconds of meeting them. Worse, we are often reluctant to let go of our initial assumptions, even in the face of contradictory evidence.

Looking for visual clues

We constantly make outrageous snap judgements about people's personalities, class, wealth, occupations, success and even sexual skills based on a minimal amount of information.

Through rapid mental gymnastics we analyze the visual information we receive about other people. We cross-reference their various visual clues with thousands of previously memorized "cards" in our visual database and produce a category for them to be slotted into, often based on ridiculous stereotypes or prejudices we learned as children and have never abandoned.

1 A woman enters a bar. What assumptions do you make about her sexuality, her availability and her attraction based simply on her appearance? What do her clothes, hair, jewelry and facial expression tell you about her?

2 She sees her friend and takes off her coat. What shifts in your set of assumptions about her? What does her smile change in your prejudice?

Gender signals

The variation in the distribution of core gender signals is endless.

Men range from "super-male" muscle-bound hulks to "effeminate" skinny waifs, while women range from curvy goddesses to the opposite poles of androgyny. Most people fall towards the center ground, but even those who fall towards the ends of the curve are still normal, but less common to us because their numbers are fewer. There are certain key physical differences between men and women that enable us to differentiate between the sexes in the space of an instant. The table below picks out some of the more obvious examples.

Her	Him
• A space and gentle mound at the apex of the legs	• A bulge at the apex of the legs
• Hips wider in relation to the waist	• Hips narrower in relation to the waist
• Narrower waist and shoulders	• Wider waist and shoulders
• Elbows closer to the body	• Elbows away from the body
• Proportionately more fat and with a different distribution	• Proportionately less fat and with a different distribution
• Buttocks protruding more	• Buttocks protruding less
• Greater buttock movement when walking	• Less buttock movement when walking
• Pronounced breasts	• Undeveloped breasts
• Smaller skeletal frame	• Larger skeletal frame (hands and feet especially)
• Muscle less massive	• Muscle more massive
• Shorter stature	• Taller stature
• Less hair on body and face	• Hairier
• Hardly discernible Adam's apple	• Prominent Adam's apple
• Softer, smoother skin	• Skin less smooth, less soft
• Higher-pitched voice	• Lower-pitched voice
• Age-related baldness rare	• Age-related baldness common
• Fleshier lips	• Less fleshy lips
• Less bushy eyebrows	• Bushier eyebrows
• More sensitive skin	• Less sensitive skin
• Shoulders and knees rounded	• Shoulders and knees less rounded

Clothes

The clothes we wear make a loud non-verbal statement about who we are, what we stand for, how much we care about our appearance and fashion trends, and how interested we are in displaying our sexuality.

The "hot" colors, especially scarlet, are all linked with sexuality. Bright red actually makes us physically aroused – breathing and heart rates rise in the presence of strong red colors. We literally warm up in a fashion similar to when we are becoming sexually turned on. The "red cape" effect is a myth when it comes to bulls, but not with humans. In one experiment, college students were shown photographs of the same woman dressed soberly or provocatively in a sexually revealing outfit. In the latter image, she was consistently judged by both men and women to be more sexually active, flirtatious, willing to use her sexuality for personal advantage and more likely to be unfaithful. This is clearly ridiculous, yet it shows that when we have no other information upon which to make sound assessments, our imaginations automatically create judgements about people that are based on nothing more than speculation.

Our imaginations play a central role in the early formation of relationships. One of the greatest turn-ons is imagining the parts of another person's body that we cannot see. Clothes that hint at what lies below the folds of material are much more exciting than show-it-all displays. A long skirt with a discreet split that occasionally reveals a flash of leg is infinitely alluring to a man. In the same way, men's clothes that suggest a fine body are usually sexier to women than skin-tight T-shirts.

Once in a relationship you may choose to dress for your partner, but initially you should dress for yourself. Wear clothes that make you feel good, enhance your best features and send a message that matches the image you want to communicate. Ask yourself how colors make you feel, and also what effect they might have on someone you want to attract.

Clothes that allow observers to "peek" at the body underneath are more attractive and exciting than flagrant displays because they invoke the imagination.

Using accessories

Everything about your clothes carries a non-verbal message, and many clothes bear verbal messages as well: designer labels and T-shirt slogans, for example, make an impression. Even the colors, the cut and the texture of clothes affect the way we are perceived by others.

In Western society we regard people's work as a significant indicator of status and personality, and we attach assumed desirability levels to careers in a hierarchical fashion. Until recently, our society was virtually uniformed. People identified their membership in particular social groups and occupations by wearing specific sets of clothes. We still assume that it is possible to guess a person's job just by judging how they are dressed. What you wear creates an immediate impression on others as well as how you feel about yourself.

Prior to the exchange of verbal information, there will be many other non-verbal clues to the status and personality of the person to whom you are attracted. Women and men alike pick up on these clues, although women are better at this particular skill than men. Non-verbal indicators include wedding rings, signet rings, diamond rings, other jewelry, watches and shoes. The latter say a great deal about us because they are at the periphery of our bodies, but they often receive the least care. How high or low are the heels? How clean are the shoes? How well made? How fashionable or traditional? Good-quality, well-made shoes are always a sign of high status, and, like it or not, the possession of perceived high status increases our sexual attraction.

We use accessories to present a particular version of ourselves. "Getting dressed to go out" is about deliberately enhancing our appearance, yet it may also be a deception or bluff. First impressions may be accurate or completely false. Like a great detective, we need to gather the clues carefully.

After lingerie, shoes are the greatest fetish. Men who complain their women have too many pairs of shoes are missing the point.

A man's watch is often his only high-value piece of jewelry. It speaks volumes about his style, status and wealth.

Power, confidence and status

If we rate someone as being highly attractive, sexy and desirable the moment we see them, we will actively discriminate in their favor.

Apart from the obvious symbols of status such as clothing and accessories, an impression of power can be created by a combination of the way we use our eyes, how comfortable we look in our bodies, how relaxed our faces appear and the degree to which our muscle tone looks firm and well-shaped. These are all things over which we have the power of change and choice.

Our body language reflects the way we feel about ourselves. The higher our self-esteem, the more comfortable we appear and the more attractive we become. Low self-esteem is a principal cause of anxiety and social discomfort. When we feel good about ourselves we tend to hold ourselves upright – not in a stiff or stretched fashion, but balanced and tall. Actual height does not matter as much as presence and vitality. The authority with which you command your own body directly affects the way you are perceived by others.

Our sexual communication skills serve us best after we confront the truth of who we are inside, integrating this into how we present ourselves to the world. The greater the congruence between inner and outer self, the more "real" our sexual relationships will be.

Initial external attraction is based on a series of highlighted gender signals and media-contrived fashions and fads, such as: big bust, small bust, short hair, long hair, heavy make-up, natural make-up.

We must work on enhancing both our sense of self internally and the image that we present to the world. Inner self-esteem grows as we enhance the way we look. Wearing something we like cheers us up. The clothes we wear, our hairstyle, the degree of care we spend in cleaning and grooming ourselves can all contribute to the way we view ourselves and other people see us.

Self-confidence survey

Take a sheet of paper and make a list of all the things you like about yourself.

This is not an incitement to be big-headed; it is to help you realize that you have a much greater chance of other people liking or loving you if you are conscious of liking or loving yourself. The more you like yourself, the more you will wear your body around you in comfort. The more comfortable you look, the more attractive you will be to others.

Handshakes

A handshake says so much about us: a handshake can have a lasting effect on the impression we make on others and the degree to which they find us attractive.

When you greet someone, do you shake hands with confidence or doubt? There's no need to squeeze the life out of another person's hand in order to impress them with your status. Similarly, shaking hands so limply that it feels as if your arm is dead is not going to give anyone the idea that you're anything but wet. Look at your hands and nails for a minute.

- What do they say about you?
- How big are they?
- What shape are they?
- How rough or soft is the skin of your palms?
- What temperature are they?

Shaking hands with a stranger is surprisingly intimate. Actually feeling the other person, we make instant judgements about their character and status. Unconsciously we reveal our desire to dominate by placing our thumb on top.

- Are they damp, and are you aware of how this changes depending on your state of emotional arousal?
- Are your nails clean and cut into a clear shape or are they dirty?
- Do you bite them?

Numerous experiments have been carried out by psychologists regarding the effects of various styles of handshake. By far the most favorable first impression made by both men and women was when the handshake lasted five seconds and was firm without being uncomfortable. Furthermore, a dry palm makes a better impression since a sweaty palm may signify nervousness. This, combined with assured eye contact, a slight smile towards the middle of the handshake moving to a wider smile at the last stage of the handshake, and a small tilt of the head to one side, forms the ultimate positive impression.

Research shows that people of high status tend to shake hands with their palms facing downwards. People less concerned with power tend to offer a hand in which the thumb is on top and may have less need of domination.

The two-hand shake can be used to communicate genuine warmth and affection but it is more often perceived as being creepy and typical of politicians concerned to "appear" sincere.

Making the first move

Traditionally, it would appear that men have always been expected to make the first move, from earliest man hunting for food to feed potential offspring or fighting rivals.

In reality women are rarely truly "passive" when they are being persuaded by potential lovers. It is usually the women who, with a subtle variety of non-verbal signals combined with higher visual accuracy and a generally elevated intuition, initiate the chase.

However, it seems things are changing. In Britain and America, especially, it is now quite common for a woman to make the first overt move, to initiate conversation and, rather than "follow," to take the physical lead in proceeding up the step-by-step ladder of non-verbal behaviors that lead to a full sexual commitment. Most cultures, though, still expect the man to apparently take the initiative while in effect following her subtle commands.

Extended eye-to-eye gazing is characteristic of intense attraction. Touching foreheads is very often a precursor to kissing.

Making a first move is no longer the preserve of men. An invitation to dance will allow physical intimacy and playfulness to develop safely.

Listen to your feelings

All too often people find that they end up with an unsuitable partner despite their intuitive reading of their own or the other person's body language.

Warning thoughts such as, "You really don't like this person, so why are you letting them kiss you?" breed not affection but self-revulsion. Listen to these warnings and act upon them. Of course, people do grow to love people over time, while "love at first sight" is sometimes lost. Nothing in life is concrete; we change in our tastes all the time.

What and who we find attractive is highly fluid – we are all friends with at least one person whom we did not like when we first met them. In the same way that first impressions about people can be completely wrong, our feelings of attraction are sometimes unreliable.

Attraction and aesthetics

The question of what we find attractive in other people and what we can do to enhance our own best assets is a major preoccupation during at least some part of our lives.

Your aesthetic intuition counts for a lot. Be careful how much you let your intrusive intellect muscle in on territory best dominated by your gut feelings. Tune into your own body language as you come close to someone of the opposite sex.

We all have expectations of people's characters and personalities and we base these on physical appearance. Research shows these expectations are usually inaccurate. We are continually bombarded with mass-media-conceived images of what is attractive, yet most of us fail to match up to these images.

The surer you are of your own likes and dislikes, the more attractive you are to others, because self-confidence is usually rated as being attractive. But remember that you are able to change your mind about other people. As you enhance your love of variety and your love affair with life, so your love of yourself will grow. By trying to be optimistic and positive you can obtain a much greater level of contentment in your life, and develop an understanding that a wider scope of what is attractive to you in other people will greatly enhance the likelihood of your meeting someone to whom you are very attracted and who is attracted to you.

Some qualities are universally attractive: happiness, a capacity for joy, play, fun, laughter, pleasure, sensual awareness, authenticity, confidence and competence. Other qualities are endlessly varied in their capacity to attract: smell, coloring, hair type, sound of voice, body shape. What matters is the ability to be true to your own aesthetic.

The eyes

Smoldering eyes; icy stare; looking daggers; if looks could kill; shifty eyes; deep eyes; eyes of an angel; piercing blue eyes; sheep's eyes; come-to-bed eyes; the evil eye or the glad eye. These are just some of the phrases used to describe the power of the glance.

Windows of the soul

The eyes are the most important tools in the successful use and understanding of sexual non-verbal communication.

Our eyes are vital both for receiving non-verbal sexual signals and sending intimate covert and overt messages straight into the consciousness of other people. The eyes do not lie. They are, some say, the windows to the soul. The more you point others to your eyes, or allow other people access to the secrets they contain, the more truthful you are being, the more confident you feel and appear, and the more encouragement you give others to access your inner thoughts, feelings and desires.

Expressive eyes

The eyes reveal everything about our erotic and romantic states. They are the most expressive part of our body. They reveal our deepest feelings and desires. Victor Hugo, in *Les Miserables*, writes eloquently on the matter:

> *The power of a glance has been so much abused in love stories that it has come to be disbelieved in. Few people dare now say that two beings have fallen in love because they have looked at each other. Yet it is in this way that love begins and in this way only. The rest is only the rest, and comes afterwards. Nothing is more real than these great shocks, which two souls give each other in exchanging this spark.*

An ancient witchcraft text describes the intensity of connection that eye-to-eye gazing engenders:

> *When your eyes be reciprocally bent one upon the other and are joined beams to beams and lights to lights, then the spirit of one is joined to the spirit of the other and strong ligations made and most violent love is stirred up with a sudden looking on, as it were, with a darting look, or piercing into the very inmost of the heart.*

Gaze for a time at her eyes and notice what feelings and thoughts are awoken in you. The power of a single gaze to change our state can be visceral.

Making the most of the eyes

Ever since the time of the ancient Minoans and Egyptians cosmetics have been used, particularly by women, to enhance the size, shape and color of the eyes.

Make-up is used all over the world to make the skin appear more youthful and the eyes more beautiful. Many legendary film stars, such as Bette Davis, have been celebrated for the color of their pupils and the shape of their eyes. In Western culture almond-shaped eyes are particularly prized.

Especially in a babyish face, large eyes show initial attraction between people of the opposite sex. This is why one of the central skills of eye flirting is to know how to make your eyes slightly larger without staring.

Eye make-up is used to highlight the whites, make their size appear larger, and alter the shape of the eye. Darkened eyelashes exaggerate the flirty potential of eyes and coloring on the eyelids can increase the apparent depth and color of the pupil.

Do men make passes…?

Some researchers allege that wearing glasses makes people less attractive, but this isn't necessarily the case. Glasses suit some people very well, especially if they use them as a beauty prop rather than a screen to hide behind. When buying glasses, choose the frames carefully to suit your face shape and get lenses that help to magnify the eyes.

Other people prefer the benefits of contact lenses, and even use colored lenses. These can have a startling effect, especially when used to enhance blue/green eyes. Other people are lucky enough to possess eyes of an unusual color. Bright green eyes are especially rare and subsequently mesmerizing, as are eyes whose irises include patches of a different color contrasting with the main iris color.

Smiling eyes

It is possible to smile with just your eyes, in the same way that it is possible for us to hear when a person is smiling on the other end of the phone. When speaking face to face we can also detect tiny changes in the many muscles around the eyes when a person smiles "inside" his or her head. Our eyes seem to become brighter when we smile; they seem to sparkle. The facial changes may be very slight but we can detect the subtlest movement and respond subconsciously by feeling more attracted to that person.

People will be more attracted to you the more you use your eyes to send out and react to unspoken messages. You will be perceived as being a more sympathetic, more expressive and more interesting person.

Smiling eyes are irresistible and central to attraction. Having a "glint" or a "twinkle" in our eyes is one of the most reliable predictors of desirability.

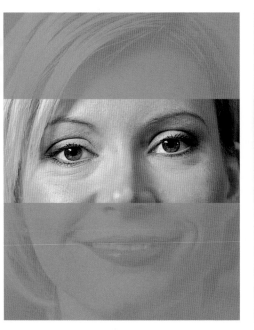
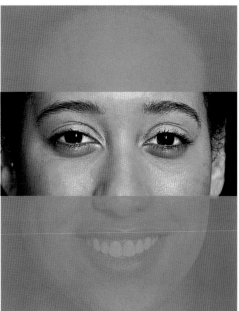

Pupil power

Michael Argyle, one of the world experts in this field, has shown that the larger our pupil size the more interested we are in what we are looking at, and that this is also a direct indicator of sexual interest and arousal.

His research confirms experiments by Hess in the early 1970s, which showed that men found photographs of women more attractive when the pupils were dilated. Likewise, women experience the same reaction.

Allow your eyes to dart backwards and forwards between these two photographs. At first glance they may seem identical, but you will almost certainly find one of the two images much more attractive than the other. Which are you more drawn to? In fact, the images are exactly the same, except that the pupils in the right-hand picture are enlarged. In real life, this dilation of the pupils, which is beyond our control, occurs when we are attracted to someone.

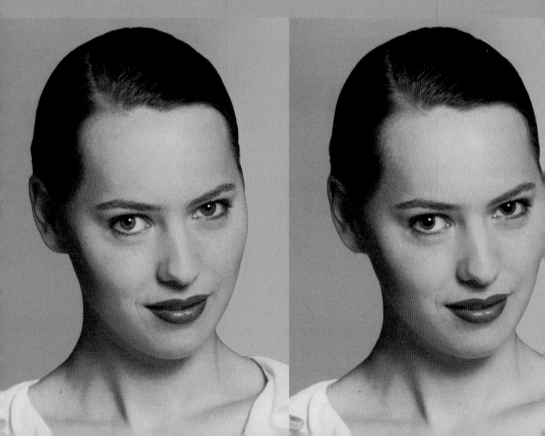

Cupid's arrows

The eyes can be used to project clear messages, and the force of your personality, over considerable distances and in very short spaces of time.

Eyes can meet briefly across an airport terminal or even at red traffic lights. It is easy to glance in your driving mirror and meet the reflected eyes of the driver behind. Such a tiny exchange can make the heart beat faster and, at its most extreme, can make even the icy-hearted feel as if they have just been kicked in the chest by a mule. Just a few seconds after visual contact, however, we go our different ways forever.

Poets and novelists have for centuries described coming under the spell of someone's looks, being bewitched and mesmerized by a single glance. We really do seem capable of catching a potential lover with just our eyes. It can happen in the most unexpected places: in the gym; passing each other on a moving escalator; in the supermarket check-out line...

So many people have regrets of missed opportunities. They fail to follow up the exchange of the initial spark, they often glance away without even returning an eyebrow flash, and then the moment has passed. If someone starts an eye conversation with you and you like their look, then answer back. You have a lot to gain and little to lose. It takes courage and confidence to respond appropriately to romantic eye contact. It is an art form that comes with repeated practice. Flirting at others with our eyes is safe, entertaining and often joyful.

Pretty woman

Italian women in the 18th century would place tiny drops of belladonna (an extract from the deadly nightshade plant) into their eyes to artificially dilate their pupils and increase their sex appeal.

Setting a romantic mood by turning down the lights partly achieves its success through the resultant pupil dilation which makes us appear simultaneously attractive and more turned-on. It has exactly the same effect on our companion. This is why candle-lit dinners are synonymous with romance – candlelight not only flatters skin color and texture, it encourages and shows off our pupil dilation to best effect.

Scanning the face

How do you follow up that first glance, to convey the idea that you're interested?

After the first burst of eye contact both parties naturally avert their gaze quite swiftly – playing an unconscious game of peek-a-boo (see page 80). When you break the initial contact you should do so by looking down. Glancing away in any other direction is less friendly, less inviting, less sexy. If you don't look away at all you can place a considerable amount of pressure upon the other person. A look that is too intense too early may be misconstrued as hostile.

Now go on to meet eyes again, scanning your target lover's eyes a couple of times and then scanning their face. They will probably scan your face similarly. Competently and sensitively done, this mutual scanning can be very pleasing, but avoid over-scanning and staring, which is very unpleasant, especially for women.

Seventy-five percent of the scan, or even more, is devoted to exploring the eyes and mouth. A normal face scan lasts about three seconds but, as with so many of the eye's sexual signals, a slight extension in duration to about four and a half seconds intensifies the emotional arousal of both parties. In the absence of any other visual cues, prolonged eye-to-eye contact is aggressive and will put the other person on their guard even if they do not know why. Therefore, if you are going to extend eye contact, remember to smile a gentle, sincere smile and accompany this with open, non-threatening hand and body signals.

Remember that there are cultural differences. North American, British and most European cultures approve of direct eye-to-eye contact and actively encourage it as a sign of confidence and strength, whereas in Eastern and West Indian cultures eye-to-eye contact tends to be avoided. In a few countries, any eye contact between a man and a woman is seen as potentially sexual and is therefore politely avoided.

Experiments tracing eye movements shows a clear scanning pattern. Our eyes dance backwards and forwards between the eyes and then include the mouth in a sweeping triangle movement.

Less frequent and wider sweeps to the extremities of the face and hair build up a complete frame of reference that is centered on the eyes and mouth. A normal face scan lasts three seconds.

Scanning the body

Women and men tend to scan each other's bodies differently. Women who are flirting are far more subtle in the way they scan a man's full image.

Wandering eyes

The human eye is so keenly attuned that if someone begins to take a visual interest in us, say from across the room at a party, we will immediately take detailed mental notes not only of how their eyes connect and disconnect with ours, but also how their eyes are behaving the rest of the time.

Many men blow their chances of connecting with a potential partner because after the initial eye-to-eye contact has been made, they get a severe case of "wandering eye," where they scan every other female in the room with the same searing red dot that the first woman might have thought was exclusively for her. "And I thought he only had eyes for me," she might think to herself before adding one more to the junk pile of male rejects. Once in a relationship, both men and women (but women especially) seem to develop an uncanny sense which enables them to detect even the merest sideways glance at another attractive member of the opposite sex.

We have the ability to detect even the briefest glance from someone sizing us up. One of the biggest causes of unease in women is when someone's gaze falls onto their breasts. A low-cut dress invites attention, but men who allow their eyes to wander in such an obvious way look very unattractive and such a gaze is unlikely to do anything except cause offense.

What they look at

Women

- Spend more time on his face, especially the mouth, eyes and hair
- Size and build
- Clothes: shoes, rings, other jewelry and watches
- Butt: this is a real turn-on for many women
- Crotch: if they're feeling overtly sexual
- Leg length: for some women, but this is not as important as it is for men

Men

- Breasts
- Leg length: this is a major visual turn-on
- Generally scans from ground up: feet, legs, crotch, torso, breasts, shoulders and then face

Men who keep their gaze focused on a woman's face rather than her body are consistently rated as being more attractive.

Scanning or leering?

Women are all too often confronted with gawking men who virtually commit eyeball assault.

It is humiliating, derogatory and unsexy for a woman to be "undressed" by a stranger's eyes. Men seem to be instinctively over-assertive and often offensive with their eyes, and many women end up feeling that men simply have conversations with their chests, or leer at their legs. His whole ground-upwards scan takes a second or less but is very off-putting and unpleasant for the woman concerned.

The eyebrow flash

Our eyebrows help to frame the eyes and give sharp definition to signals we send with our eyes by accentuating any movement of the surrounding muscles.

When we first see somebody across a room to whom we are attracted, we respond automatically with an eyebrow flash when that person looks our way. The whole event normally lasts about a fifth of a second, during which our eyebrows will rise and fall, followed instantly by a return eyebrow flash from the other person. If someone wants to create a deliberate effect, they may make it last for up to a second.

We use the eyebrow flash only when we wish to acknowledge another person's presence, as it is a signpost to a following exchange. If we don't want to acknowledge an eyebrow flash from someone we simply ignore it or pull our eyebrows into a disapproving frown. Eyebrow flashes are also used in conjunction with a roll of the eyes to indicate exasperation, but the duration of the flash is usually longer than the warm "greeting" flash.

In any potentially friendly exchange or meeting you should learn to initiate an eyebrow flash and be aware that returning an eyebrow flash across a room will send a clear message of good intent. However, range is important. At a distance of less than 5 feet, the flash takes on a less agreeable feel, while at a distance of 14 feet or more, the other person may not even be aware of your flash.

The eyebrow flash is an instantly recognized non-verbal signal of friendly greeting practiced in every corner of the globe. Because it is so universal, researchers claim that this gesture is an inborn response. As the eyebrows rise to their peak, the eyeballs are exposed because the eyelids lift and the muscles around the eyes stretch, allowing more light on to the surface of the eyes. This makes them appear large and bright and is very attractive.

To stare or to gaze?

Staring and gazing are not at all the same thing: one is attacking and the other inviting.

A stare is like shooting invisible arrows from our eyes and into the eyes of the person on the receiving end, leaving them cold or feeling invaded. A gaze, however, welcomes a person into our line of sight and into our eyes. The person upon whom we gaze feels great warmth. Women generally gaze more than men. This may be because they are often more attentive listeners too. Women will find the eyes of a man who gazes well very attractive, the more so because many men are unskilled at this.

Gazing for best effects

When you meet someone in whom you are interested, look them in the eye as they begin to speak. When they want you to speak they will probably pause for a moment. Don't ignore this signal – it is a cue for you to pick up the conversation. The most effective gaze pattern is to make regular furtive glances with intervals of about three to five seconds between, increasing to every two to three seconds as interest develops.

We know that two people in love spend ages gazing into each other's eyes. You can bring about this desirable "mutual lovers' gaze" with a relative stranger if you can successfully draw another's look into the center of your own eyes.

The eyebrows are full of expression and essential for sexual flirtation. They allow us to communicate everything from disapproval or disbelief to excitement, arousal and desire.

Inviting the gaze in

Women generally find doing this much simpler, as men are easy prey to a deep, hypnotic gaze. Give any man a dreamy, five-second burst of gazing and his toes will curl, his heart will flush, and he will become putty in a woman's hands.

When men try the same thing, they usually blow it because they have a greater tendency to stare. They come on with a visual onslaught far too strong. If a woman is shy or wary of intimate eye contact, the last thing she needs is for a man to look at her even more; it will frighten her. A man in this case should back off, turn the eye-heat right down, copy the woman's more furtive eye glances, enjoy the hide-and-seek game of sneaked looks and flashing glances, and build up slowly to the long gaze.

We make ourselves even more inviting by using our hands as pointers to draw the gaze of another person into our own gaze path. The pointer can be floating in mid-air, or actually touching our face; it doesn't have to be our fingers or hands – we can also point with pens and cigarettes, with pipes or glasses. Eyes automatically follow a moving hand, locking onto the powerful "magnet" signal being beamed out from the center of our eyes.

Much of human motivation is based on reward and fulfillment. Classical models of reinforcement show that it is possible to highlight another person's impression of us as attractive and sexy by reinforcing eye contact with something else pleasurable. So, for example, as we point to our eyes we should also smile and, if circumstances allow for it, say something flattering about the person upon whom we have fixed our eyes. If you are blessed with the ability to make others laugh, then do so as you point to your eyes for maximum reinforcement. The person upon whom your attention is fixed will experience a warm feeling inside and associate that feeling with a direct and intimate connection with you.

No matter what your expression may be, your eyes possess great power and influence. When you have finished reading this chapter, your increased awareness of your eyes will have increased their power. As soon as you can, get out onto the university of the street and you will see for yourself the immense sexual allure of the eyes.

Let your eyes glance between the two faces. Notice how your own emotions are changed by his expression, staring and full of intensity, compared to hers, which is so much more open, gazing, seductive and inviting.

Blinking and winking

The rate at which we blink has a profound unconscious effect on anyone looking at or into our eyes.

As adults we blink once every two to three seconds, on average. If we don't think consciously about blinking, our lids move at a very fast rate. Normally we don't notice our own or other people's blink rates. If the norm is diverted from, however, our supersense detects it immediately.

In marked contrast, some people close their eyes for extended periods of time during conversation. Desmond Morris labelled this phenomenon as "cut-off" behavior. Someone doing this excludes all visual stimulation, and in so doing excludes anyone who might wish to communicate with them, which can be insulting and unattractive.

To induce a romantic feel, however, by all means blink. If someone looks at us eye-to-eye and is very attracted to us, their pupil size will increase (see page 68) and they will unconsciously blink more rapidly. If you blink more often your-self, the person you are talking to (if they like you) will unconsciously try to match your blink rate. This will in turn make you both feel attracted to each other.

A man winking as a method of commun-icating sexual interest is almost always a mistake. For the most part, men wink so rarely that when they do, it looks awkward or exaggerated.

Winks

The wink is a fantastically powerful sexual signal when it is used by women, but can often be something of a turn-off when used by men. The "nudge, nudge, wink, wink" overtones of a group of men sharing a dirty joke is a sad perversion of the original meaning – a knowing wink signifies a shared secret, something special and thrilling because of its covert quality.

Men can use winks to send a clear message of sexual intent towards a woman, but they are best delivered with subtlety. The "quieter" the wink, the more pleasing it is to receive. Delivered in conjunction with a gentle smile, it can be devastating.

As with most non-verbal sexual signals, women are more skilled at delivering such messages. A wink from a woman can have a dramatic effect upon a man. He will usually interpret the signal as an overt invitation, so use it with care!

Eyelashes

Eyelashes focus the gaze upon the eyes, which is why fluttering eyelashes are considered so flirtatious and why men with very long or very dark eyelashes are often considered very attractive by women.

The two-eyed wink

When a blink mimics a wink it becomes sexual without being corny or leering.

This is done by blinking in slow motion, consciously slowing down the rate of your blink to a half or a third of the natural speed. Both men and women seem to find the effect very attractive. It is especially potent if done as follows.

• Start by looking away from the person you wish to flirt with.

• When you sense they are looking at you, cast your eyes towards theirs, meeting their gaze.

• Hold still for about three seconds, then blink very slowly and then smile as you reopen your eyes.

• Wait for them to smile in response and then look away again. The whole sequence should last about seven seconds.

Peek-a-boo

Peek-a-boo was one of our first and favorite games in life and it is reflected in many adult non-verbal sexual signals.

As babies we loved it when adults teased us by alternately hiding and revealing their eyes, squealing and giggling with delight every time the eyes reappeared as if by magic, so peek-a-boo is one of the first games we learned that taught us the excitement of anticipation. The longer the eyes were concealed the greater the tension and the more pleasurable the relief when concealment was removed to reveal smiling eyes

The two-eyed wink described on page 79 is so effective because it is a miniature peek-a-boo event. In adulthood peek-a-boo is seldom actually played with the hands; instead, we use other objects to deliberately conceal our eyes. In past times, ladies used fans to dramatic sensual effect by hiding their eyes behind eyelash-like fluttering feathered fans, raising and lowering them provocatively. This movement, combined with the eyebrow flash and then the lowering of the eyes, could be breathtaking. At the classic masked ball, hand-held masks are raised and lowered in a teasing cat-and-mouse manner.

Peek-a-boo can be played anywhere: on the bus, peeking over a newspaper; in the library, over a book; in an art gallery, peering around the sides of a large piece of sculpture; in a club or a bar, peeking around a pillar; even in a crowd, using other people to obscure the line of vision.

So peek-a-boo can be exciting, arousing, entertaining, laugh-inducing, flirtatious and even highly erotic. You've probably been playing your own version of it for years and just never realized it.

Peek-a-boo is harmless, sensous, and can be downright sexy. Long hair is wonderful for masking an eye; it is then possible – and very alluring – to play peek-a-boo by covering and uncovering just one eye.

We play peek-a-boo with potential mates with myriad subtle gestures and moments in which we manipulate other people or objects, such as sunglasses, to allow us to make momentary eye contact. Peeking around other people can be explosively provocative, because the desire to re-establish eye contact is almost irresistible.

The mouth

Mouths are almost as complex as eyes. A large percentage of our brain is allocated to interpreting signals from and directing the behavior of our lips and tongue. We often define people's characters according to their mouths, describing them with expressions such as tight-lipped or loudmouthed, or as having a stiff upper lip, a false smile, a Bardot pout, a Cheshire cat grin, a sensuous mouth or hot lips.

Sexy mouth and shape

Why are some mouths seen as sexy and others not?
What messages does your mouth give out about you?

Are your lips narrow and colorless, fleshy and soft, firm and dark, or cracked and chapped? Are they quite evenly shaped or very asymmetrical? Do you bite them a lot, and, if you do, does it look attractive when you do it? Do you touch your lips a lot with your fingers, or other objects like pens? Do you love playing with chewing gum in your mouth? Do you get a lot of comfort from your mouth by biting your nails, sucking your thumb or gnawing a knuckle? Are you very sensuous when it comes to tasting your food and drink? Do you savor tastes in a sexual way? Have you learned to smell using your mouth and tongue as a powerful addition to your nose?

If the eyes of a man or woman to whom you are attracted meet yours, his or her lips will automatically part for a moment if the attraction is mutual. This movement is often very subtle. At the extreme, someone who is very sexy can literally take your breath away!

Remember, don't hide your mouth, especially your smile. All too often we bring our hands up to cover our mouths, such as to stifle a laugh, and in doing so we hide one of our most precious assets. The eyes act as searchlights to pinpoint our gaze on others and as flares to attract attention. Once someone's eyes are upon you, direct their gaze into your eyes and towards your mouth and lips. All human beings scan faces in a triangular motion between the eyes and the lips, so do not interfere with this natural pattern. Use it to your advantage; do not hide your mouth, point at it instead.

Everything we put into or near our mouth has the potential to be suggestive of sexual intent. Some foods like ice cream can be particularly sensual.

Pouting lips are sexy because they invite kissing, and because they simulate the enlargement of the aroused female sexual organs.

Smiles

It is usually the mouth that reveals a person's real mood.
A false smile is a dead giveaway and is easily spotted.

Smiles come in hundreds of forms and degrees of intensity, yet whether
it is a big grin or a shy flicker of a smile we are somehow able to detect it
when someone is not using the risorious muscle – that is to say, when
the feelings and thoughts in someone's head are not conducive to smiling.
The insincere smile is given away most noticeably by asymmetry. The smile
is one-sided, frequently looks exaggerated and is held in a fixed position for
too long. The lower lip moves less than the upper, as if it had been frozen,
and, most importantly, the eyes refuse to cooperate with the false actions
of the lips.

One of the principal reasons so many people fail in their attempts to
use non-verbal communication to attract or impress members of the
opposite sex is that, without realizing it, they spend most of their time
looking miserable.

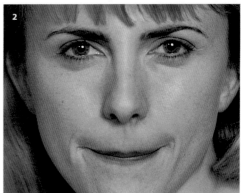

1 The closed-mouth
smile, when natural,
is used normally when we
are smiling to ourselves.
But here it is slightly lopsided, which indicates
insincerity.

2 The tight-lipped
smile, also known as
the miserable smile, often
indicates suppressed
anger or pain.

At first glance these smiles may appear to be very similar, but look again more closely. Each conveys its own distinct message. See how the smile spreads across the face and eyes in some and not others.

3 The full or broad smile is symmetrical. The laughter lines begin to appear on the face and around the eyes.

4 A false smile is indicated by the tight jaw and top lip, cold, slightly narrowed eyes and lack of laughter lines.

A genuine smile activates not only the risorius muscle but also the arbicularis oculi, the muscle that causes our cheeks to rise and draws in the skin around the eye sockets, causing crinkling at the outer corners of the eyes. The real smile is well-rounded, with happy lines extending out across the whole face, including the forehead, which becomes less creased, and the eyebrows, which flatten out or rise up.

Both men and women (but more so women) tend to bare their teeth as they become very aroused sexually. This expression of a primitive, aggressive, adrenaline-driven state of sexual arousal links *Homo sapiens* to the other primates. A tight-lipped or closed-mouth smile is less sensuous. A smirk or sly grin is an almost guaranteed turn-off, as is a very immobile smile.

Smiling has a dramatic effect on our feelings and our physiology. Just pulling our face muscles into a big smile makes us feel better. "But won't that be a fake smile?" you might ask: the answer is yes and no. A fake smile held for long enough can actually make us feel more positive and think more optimistic and happy thoughts, which will in turn cause a real smile. The process can be thought-led too. By focusing your mind on a funny smile-inducing thought to the exclusion of depressing thoughts you can bring a smile to your face.

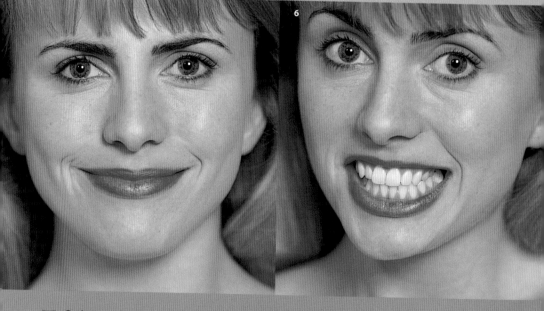

5 During sexual arousal the lips swell and darken in color. Colored lipsticks simultaneously hide this natural change and mimic it; dark reds suggest a state of permanent arousal.

6 An exaggerated full-teeth smile can be hostile, especially when the teeth are clenched. Here the smile is also one-sided, like an insincere politician's smile.

Pleasurable thoughts tend to evoke smiles. You should never suppress a smile as it will be one of your most attractive assets, whatever your looks. We are automatically attracted to smiling faces and we smile back involuntarily in response to a smile greeting. You have the ability right now to make yourself more sexually attractive simply by choosing to smile more. The ability to make others smile and laugh is sexy. Part of our attraction motivation is naturally selfish; we like to imagine what the person we are eyeing up will bring us in terms of pleasure rewards. Smiling a lot scores very high on the unconscious pleasure-principle selection scoreboard.

Laughter is even more therapeutic and sexy than smiling. When you laugh you release a variety of natural drugs into the bloodstream that give pleasure and relaxation.

Examine your lips in a mirror. Notice every detail and think what you can do to enhance their appearance. Using lip balm is an easy way to enhance the appeal of your lips.

7 A genuine happy smile lights up the whole face. The eyes smile and sparkle, the cheekbones lift, the smile lines around the eyes and mouth are obvious and the jaw muscles are relaxed. Research shows that regular smiling can lift depression by releasing chemicals into the brain that change our mood.

8 The pouting smile is an overtly sexual invitation to a kiss.

Fake and genuine smiles

Compare the man in these two photographs – which of them do you find more genuine?

The insincere smile is given away most noticeably by asymmetry. The smile is one-sided, frequently looks exaggerated and is held in a fixed position for too long. The lower lip moves less than the upper, as if it had been frozen, and, most importantly, the eyes refuse to cooperate with the false actions of the lips.

The complex muscles of the face help us to interpret the messages smiles send us. It is easy to see at once that this smile is anything but a friendly one. The face is taut, the head angle awkward, the smile lopsided, the eyes too intense and staring, the jaw clenched, the muscles normally used in natural smiling in this instance are over-employed.

Combining a broad symmetrical smile with an open-palm hand greeting sends a very warm non-threatening message. Adding open body language signals to this already winning combination makes us almost irresistibly attractive.

The smile as a warm greeting is as infectious as it is attractive. A glowing natural smile has a potent effect: it makes us feel better emotionally, more relaxed, more confident, more optimistic and hopeful. It makes the recipient or even passive witness of our smile feel good inside too.

Enhancing the lips

Because the lips are such strong forces in non-verbal sexual signalling, we often seek to bring them to extra attention.

Pigments applied to the lips have been used to enhance feminine beauty for at least 5000 years. Men have also historically decorated their mouths, but not to the same extent as women. As with other cosmetics, coloring the lips sends a non-verbal signal of sexual arousal which evokes a particularly strong reaction in men. Greater blood flow to the lips means that both sexes get red lips when aroused but it tends to be only women who wear lip color. This is thought to lend weight to the idea that coloring the lips mimics the reddening that occurs in the labia just before orgasm and so conveys a strong signal that a woman is turned on.

Wet lips

In the same way, wet lips seem to mimic the increased lubrication of the female genitals during sexual arousal. Thus many lipsticks and glosses are shiny to make the lips appear wet. Licking the lips is at the extreme end of non-verbal sexual signalling with the mouth and tongue. When exaggerated, it looks lecherous and uninviting, but done subtly, it sends a clear unspoken message of attraction. Try licking your lips while the other person is visually distracted or by shielding your mouth with your hand for a moment so that you're not being too obvious.

The most effective technique is to wet the lips slightly using the darting tip of the tongue.

Swollen lips

Whatever the shape of your lips, their volume increases when you become sexually aroused. Blood causes them to engorge, increasing their sensitivity dramatically as if preparing them for kissing, and again mimicking the female genitals when aroused.

The color and shape of the lips can be changed dramatically with make-up. Some men find watching a woman apply lipstick very arousing in itself.

Touching

As we become attracted to someone our lips and mouth become increasingly sensitive to touch and other stimulation.

Thus a man or woman standing at a bar eating a savory snack will, without realizing it, take even bigger mouthfuls and chew faster as they become aroused. People will actually touch their own mouths more, indicating that they may wish to speak to you and/or kiss you, as well as giving themselves pleasure by stimulating their own sensitized and full lips.

Inviting

There can be few more directly sexual non-verbal communications than the signals being displayed by this woman.

The combination of the raised shoulder, the tilted head, the sideways glance, the pouting lips and the phallic sunglasses provocatively slipped into her open mouth indicate sexual arousal and suggest that this is caused by the presence of someone she finds highly attractive. This combination of sexual signals is exploited regularly in advertising posters and commercials. It is also used by men, but to a lesser degree as the effect seems to be less powerful on women.

Kissing

A kiss is one of the most intimate and sensual non-verbal sexual signals that we have at our disposal. The way we kiss someone the first time may have a direct effect on whether the relationship continues.

What a difference it makes if you actually kiss someone's cheek when it is offered to you. Normally, if you are being introduced to someone at a social occasion you shake them by the hand, but on departing it is quite acceptable to kiss goodbye. Normally the kiss is to the air, but if it is to the cheek, it is brief, about three-quarters of a second touching time. If you extend this touching time by just half a second to one and a quarter seconds the non-verbal message is clear: "I like you and I want to kiss you lots more!"

How to be a good kisser!

Never try to force too intimate a kiss on someone too soon. The kisses you share should progress slowly so that you are both at ease as well as turned on. If you attempt to kiss someone full on the lips before he or she is ready, you may force him or her to retreat or turn awkwardly away, offering you a cheek at best. Alternatively, you may find yourself encountering a tightened jaw and tense lips. Ideally, then, the progression starts out as follows:

* First kiss gently on the lips, mouth closed.
* Then slowly let the kisses become firmer with the mouth still closed.
* Then part your lips slightly, as this allows you to smell each other's breath and taste each other's saliva, both of which carry a great deal of information, including secretions from the sebaceous glands which indicate the state of arousal. You can also feel the warmth of your co-kisser's breath.
* As passion increases part your lips further, literally opening yourselves up to each other.

Since the lips and tongue are very sensitive to temperature, warmth is a sure signal of sexual arousal. Cold skin and lips, however, are a definite indication to slow down and back off.

Dos and don'ts

The breath and saliva are important non-verbal messengers. Ideally you should offer the person you are going to kiss a biological message as unadulterated as possible.

Do
- Make sure that your teeth are clean
- Ensure that your breath is healthy and natural
- Avoid garlic

Don't
- Smoke
- Use breath freshener, toothpaste or mouthwash just before you kiss
- Drink too much
- Rush too soon into over-hard or French kisses

Strong scents and flavors such as smoke, toothpaste, beer and garlic disguise who you are sexually like a blanket dropped over your head. The sebaceous glands located in the mouth and in the corners of the lips release semiochemicals, which are highly stimulating sexually. The combination of this stimulation, which is very intoxicating and pleasurable, together with our own unique saliva "fingerprint," is the most sensual way of exchanging personal credentials. We usually know if we are going to be suited to each other physically after the first full kiss.

Learn to lip read

As passion increases we part our lips further. Men tend to rush this stage, pushing their lips hard onto their partner's, sticking their tongue into her mouth, invading her body space. Male and female individual preferences vary greatly so you should not assume that someone likes to be kissed in the same way as you do. The strong, passionate kiss is a real turn-on for some people, but you should go gently and explore first – your partner will show you by example how he or she likes being kissed if you allow the time for it. Tune your lips into your partner's and read what they are telling you. The messages can include: too fast; too strong; deeper; less pressure; more teeth; nibble my lower lip; suck my tongue; lick my teeth; play sword-fights with my tongue; make your tongue soft; make your tongue hard; show me how you will give me oral sex when we make love. All these different messages are possible and more.

Kissing can and should be a totally sensory experience. It is also, probably, the most intimate connection two people can make. It deserves thoughtful consideration, practice and sensitivity.

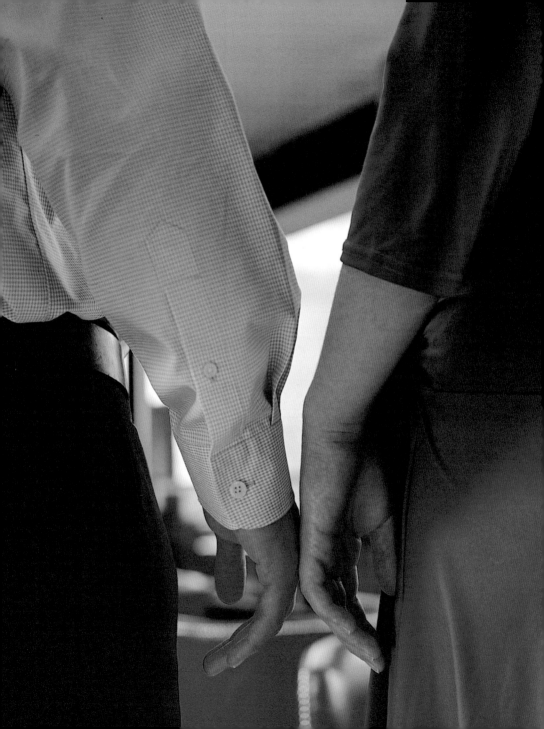

Body talk

Hold your head up and people look at you; slouch and they look away. The posture and orientation of the head and shoulders and torso speaks volumes about your personality. The bearing of your upper body makes the difference between attraction and repulsion, either drawing people to you or resolutely pushing them away.

The head, face and ears

Our face is the principal asset upon which we are judged by others as attractive or not and the principal stage upon which we act out our feelings and thoughts for others to see.

If we are attracted towards someone we indicate this with our head. We turn our face towards them. We nod at them, and even if this is a very small movement, it will be detected. If someone is talking to you, the more you respond to their speech with nods, the more they will be encouraged to continue talking, and the more they will enjoy being in your company.

We point with our heads too, often in conjunction with numerous other face and hand gestures. We can indicate direction, or signal to someone that we are interested in further contact. Since we tend to store tension, anxiety and stress around the neck and shoulders, flexibility in these parts shows that a person is at ease. A person with a stiff posture is simply less sexy.

Avoid holding your head in one fixed position: this is disconcerting. Be aware of the messages your head is conveying: if you are sticking your chin out, dropping it low, tilting your head back too far, clenching your jaw or grinding your teeth, you will appear anxious or angry.

The gentle face of love

When we are sexually attracted to someone our face changes. The skin tends to sag less under the eyes, and all the facial muscles generally tone up. Women's skin appears softer and more youthful – the "glow" of being in love. Sexual arousal also brings a flush of color into a woman's cheeks and a high degree of arousal may produce a blush on the neck, shoulders and chest.

Men often touch their faces more than they normally do when they catch sight of a woman they find attractive. They may stroke their cheeks, touch their ears, finger their neck on the front and sides, and hold their head higher and more upright. Their eyes may also appear to be brighter and more "alive."

Women stroke each part of their necks more, and touch their mouths and lips with their fingertips. They also hold their heads up more, and their eyes seem more sparkling.

The ears

Everyone's ears are different and there are no fixed stereotypes for sexy ears. What does matter is how you use them.

The greatest simple communication skill is that of being a good listener. It is the non-verbal response to speech. Men are apt to talk mainly about themselves when trying to make a good impression on women they find attractive. They also frequently talk at, rather than with, the woman and while they may ask questions they then demonstrate lack of interest in her views by ignoring the answers.

Ears have a vital role to play in seduction. They will bring you information about the person you are listening to, both in terms of verbal and non-verbal language. At least 30 percent or more of our understanding of what people say depends on the sound of their voice, rather than on the words that are actually spoken. Research into the non-verbal parts of speech shows that we make many assumptions about a person from the tone, speed, breathiness and musicality of the voice – including how sexy the person is.

Many non-verbal gestures are complex. Here the flirtatious touching of the hair, the wrist and neck display combine with the touching of the ear. Sometimes we unconsciously touch a part of our body which is normally only touched in an intimate setting, revealing that we are imagining the other person touching us.

Hair

Our hair is one of the main aspects of our appearance that we can deliberately manipulate to create an impression, whether it's by having long tresses, designer stubble or by changing its color.

Some women love men with beards or moustaches; others seem to regard clean-shaven men as sexier, although designer stubble is regarded by others as ruggedly masculine and, therefore, attractive. Similarly, men may have preferences for long or short hair.

Individual and cultural differences exist with regard to body hair too. Some cultures favor women who are almost hairless, while others are turned on by women whose bodies are very hairy, including the legs, armpits and genital regions. Some women like their men with hairy chests, while others prefer chests as smooth and bare as a baby's.

Grooming and preening

What really matters is that your hair is clean, well-groomed and in good condition. These simple things send a message of self-regard, self-confidence and good health.

Hair preening always accompanies sexual arousal. Men and women automatically touch their hair when they are attracted to someone, when they wish to make themselves look more sexy and when they want to communicate interest in another person. The hair stroke and hair flick are used equally by both sexes but provoke a stronger response when they are enacted by women. Of particular potency is the following gesture: the woman uses her hands to hold her hair up on top of her head, while glancing sideways and distinctly raising the shoulder that is nearest to the object of her desire.

Men who are in the presence of a woman whose hair is tied up, or tucked inside some kind of hat, should take note if she looks in their direction as she lets it down and flicks her hair. This particular preening gesture often accompanies sexual interest from a woman.

Stereotypes

The color of hair sends a strong signal too.

There is no scientific evidence to support any of the hair color stereotypes, but we may be affected by these stereotypes in such a way as to influence our self-perception as well as our perception of others. Blondes are reputed to have more fun.

Blonde women are often associated with sexuality and party-loving personalities and blonde women certainly receive much more direct sexual attention from men than brunettes. Blonde men are taken less seriously and, like red-headed men, are probably believed less. Black- and brown-haired women are often thought of as more serious; dark-haired men are traditionally assumed to be more romantic than the average and red-headed women are presumed to have tempers to match their fiery hair color, but again these stereotypes are based on myth.

The hair twirl indicates interest and arousal and is also an unconscious preening gesture. It is often flirtatious and can be very erotic.

We touch our hair whenever we are in the presence of someone we are attracted to, often without realizing we are revealing our feelings.

Neck and shoulders

Our neck and shoulders are far more expressive parts of our body than many of us realize.

The neck

A stiff neck has a bad effect on our general sense of well-being, confidence and emotional arousal. It will also negatively alter our entire body posture. The neck is a vulnerable and sensitive area. The muscles surrounding the spinal cord need to be relaxed and correctly positioned for us to be most finely tuned to non-verbal communications. Fear is capable of making the hairs on the back of the neck literally stand on end. On the other hand, if we find someone very attractive our neck hairs will be soft and down-like, and we may experience a pleasurable tingling sensation too. Some women have an erogenous zone on their spine six vertebrae down from the skull. To invite someone to touch your neck shows trust and is very intimate. The neck is one part of us that we normally reserve for our lovers alone.

While we frequently lean forward towards someone we feel drawn to, another gesture of sexual interest is to tilt the head back to reveal the neck and throat more openly. Both men and women do this, although men seem to respond more to the signal. The skin of the throat is often very soft and the rounded contours of the muscles mimic the more sexual areas of our bodies. Baring the throat may be the remnant of a primitive submissive gesture, seen in the behavior of many animals, where the neck and belly are exposed in deference to a dominant member of the same species or a potential attacker. There is a possible link between this and the human male's sexual appreciation of long necks. It is worth noting that many women's clothes are fashioned to highlight or enhance neck length.

Most neck jewelry has sexual implications. A single pendant, a pearl necklace, an erotic choker – all draw attention to the throat area. The skin of the throat often shows flushes of color when the woman is aroused.

Here a woman runs her fingers through her hair and tilts her head back to reveal the full extent of her neck. Meanwhile she maintains eye contact and smiles, all signals indicating her desire to be approached. Her head is angled to one side, a flirtatious and often arousing position which also indicates that she is listening carefully to what he is saying. It is also a gesture of submission.

The shoulders

When we meet someone we like, not only do we give him or her an eyebrow flash (see page 74), we also give them a shoulder flash! Without realizing it, men and women shrug their shoulders when they find each other attractive. The movement is small and rapid but if you notice that the person facing you does it, you know they are attracted to you, perhaps even before they are aware of it themselves.

The flexibility and visibility of human shoulders and the fact that they are moved by emotionally sensitive muscles renders them highly expressive. Their size and angular silhouette when squared bespeak dominance.

Shoulders are also very sensuous – hence the power of "off-the-shoulder" dresses or shirts. When a woman's shoulder is exposed and she is aroused she will often caress her shoulder with her hand or hair.

In most men the shoulders form the widest part of the torso. As such, they are often employed, deliberately or unconsciously, to act as a wall to fend off other men from approaching a woman, at a bar, for example, or else attempt to "block in" a woman. Shoulder blocking is an overt show of strength which is not necessarily going to put a woman at ease.

Hunched or lopsided shoulders suggest a lack of symmetry in the body and mind. Good posture that is balanced and upright is always considered attractive because it indicates health and, more importantly, a relaxed demeanor. This in turn suggests confidence and status.

The revealed or partly revealed shoulder is often highly arousing. It is an extension of the neck display and suggests the soft roundness of the breast.

The classic shoulder block is usually employed by men as an aggressive defense or power play. This woman's body language clearly indicates her intention to keep the second man involved in the dialogue.

Arms

The hands and arms can also signal either positive or negative feelings about someone coming on to us. How do you deal with other people's negative body language?

It is possible to indicate lack of interest by building a blockade with our arms or hands. We can literally shut someone out by covering our eyes with our hands. We can block our body protectively by folding our arms fully tensed, with our fists clenched or flat.

When we are receiving unwanted advances we tend to grip our forearms with our hands and tense our shoulders, hug ourselves around the waist, or partially protect ourselves with one arm across our body, touching the opposite side at the shoulder or the neck. If someone adopts a defensive position in response to an approach from you, take the message and change your behavior. Smile more and give them extra room. Change your posture and position in relation to them and see if you can break their barriers down by offering a hand to shake, or a glass to hold. Once you've broken through, use positive non-hostile non-verbal signalling and see if the barrier stays down. If it does, your presence is no longer being completely rejected.

Everything about the woman reveals her discomfort. His arm against the wall is an aggressive territorial display, his torso leaning towards her is an invasion of her space zone, his leg thrust forwards, his hand in his pocket and his smug smirk are all typical mistakes men make. She folds her arms, raises her left shoulder protectively, and points her feet away from him.

Missing out

Did you know that crossing your arms reduces your overall sensory intake? It really does create a shield.

If, for example, you watch a film with your arms folded you will remember less of the film than if you had sat with an open body position! You may habitually be shutting out a good deal of the potential pleasure in life just by crossing your arms. Check how often you do adopt such a position, and try unfolding your arms to feel what a difference it makes.

Of course many people fold their arms because they feel cold or because they have back pain. Folded arms do not always indicate defense, but they often suggest a person is more focused on their internal thoughts than the external world. It is also a posture of resting the arms, which are surprisingly heavy limbs.

The arms can be used to create a warm and welcoming feeling in another person. His right arm shows the way and his left arm and hand shield and guide her gently. His open palm faces her back but, crucially, does not touch her. Were his hand to touch her back, she would perceive this as an invasion of her intimate space.

Hands

Our hands perform three main roles in sexual non-verbal communication. They touch, point and signal.

We use our hands for a great many gestures too, to illustrate, dramatize and punctuate points in our conversation. We can draw in the air with them, imitate, animate and parody movement, and indicate when we wish to speak or when we want to invite someone else to speak to us. We can even call a crowd to silence just by touching a finger to our lips.

Pointing

As children we are taught not to point at people because it's rude, but as adults we still like pointing at things we want. Just imagine you are feasting your eyes on a dessert menu in a restaurant. You point at the most delicious-sounding chocolate gateaux and say, "I'll have some of that, please!" Well, the same is true when it comes to sex. We love to point at the object of our sexual desire and at our own best assets as part of our courtship ritual. We can use a pointing signal over a long distance, especially in conjunction with a smile, an eyebrow flash and a four-second eye gaze. We also point more subtly, vaguely motioning in someone's direction, perhaps holding a glass or using our entire hand.

In conjunction with moving our arms, we can point towards someone in such a way as to invite them to join us or to indicate that we are having a conversation about them. We often point and signal simultaneously; we beckon people towards us with a sweeping motion of a cupped hand, or with just one finger hooked and moving backwards and forwards, making the gesture of scratching a little in the air.

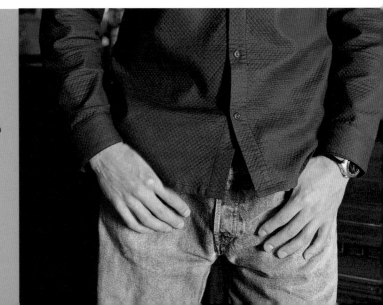

The cowboy stance is usually aggressive when used by men talking to other men – a subtle form of clashing horns. It is rarely deliberately employed. Most men take up this posture when they want to be noticed or if they are looking at a woman they find attractive. It can look ridiculous if the rest of the body language fails to live up to the sexual confidence suggested by the crotch point.

Clasping the face in both our hands is often very cute-looking. It is something we do much more as children. It is another example of a gesture that communicates our desire to be touched.

By pointing with one hand, which is apparently supporting her head, this woman is drawing us towards her gaze. This gesture increases the likelihood of initiating an intimate and extended eye exchange, which in turn leads to increased arousal and attraction.

Clean, fresh-smelling, well-cared-for hands and nails are aesthetic in men and women equally. Feeling good about our hands means we are less likely to hide them. Consequently we will communicate more effectively and create a better impression.

The cowboy stance

Often, without realizing it, we point at our genitals. This is a very sexually charged non-verbal signal and is more often performed by men.

Crotch-pointing can be overt or implied. Even a hand pushed into a pocket is suggestive, as the viewer's eye is automatically drawn down the arm in search of the hand. The "cowboy" stance can take various forms. The thumbs can be hooked into the tops of the trousers, the belt, a belt loop or the pockets and anywhere from one finger to four may do the actual pointing. We may also rest one or both hands on the hips to point towards the genitals.

Hand and arm signals

When we greet someone we often shake hands. A firm handshake is desirable for both men and women, but a handshake any longer than five seconds will imply a desire for greater intimacy.

A gentle tug can signal attraction and even the subtlest squeeze on the fleshy part of the palm can make a person of either sex want to have you hold his or her hand. If you lean gently forwards as you shake hands, it will increase your mutual state of arousal and will make your intentions clear. The unsubtle palm scratch of your opposite's hand with your middle finger is not recommended.

We can signal high status or supreme confidence – although it can be dangerously near the edge of unattractive arrogance – by placing our hands behind (not on top of) our head. The finger steeple is also a sign of great confidence. If you are lucky enough to have beautiful hands and fingernails, show these off as much as possible by using plenty of hand movements when you communicate. The possession of nice hands is rated very highly among physical attributes.

We use our hands to signal interest in someone by moving them into another's personal space. We edge our hands forward across the surface of a table or bar. We reveal our open palms towards the person we desire as a peaceful gesture of good will. An open palm is friendly and can be very inviting.

The wrists have always been considered highly erotic, especially on women, and the display of the wrist is highly suggestive and arousing. Many women put perfume on their wrists, as well as behind their ears.

Often very suggestively, although unintentionally, we use our hands to caress inanimate objects, especially wine glasses and cutlery. These are usually phallic in shape and may hint at sexual acts which we may or may not be daydreaming about. We can even use our hands, and especially our fingers, to mimic oral sex, sucking and licking food from them.

The hands and fingers illustrate and enliven our words with movements and gestures that can bring words to life and reveal much about mood and character.

1 Hands and arms emphasize and animate speech and can also send signals of attraction and sexual intent. Open-palm gestures are warm and attractive. Here the man's hands are animated and pointing. It is as if a physical line were extending from the ends of his fingertips to form a wall on either side of the woman, drawing her in and excluding others at the same time.

2 A hand extended towards someone acts as a pointer in the direction of the person to whom we are attracted. In this case the hand on the table also crosses over into the man's personal space.

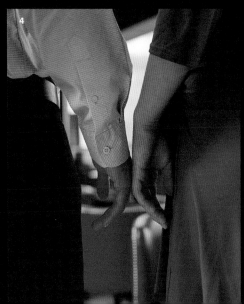

3 The wrist display is a particularly alluring and very feminine gesture. Exaggerated wrist displays and limp-wrist gestures are used by drag artists to emphasize their femininity.

4 This couple is walking so close that every so often the backs of their hands touch for a moment. What happens next is crucial. If either person wishes they can withdraw their hand to another position ensuring no further touching occurs. Otherwise they can ensure the touch is repeated. This often leads to holding hands.

Chest and breasts

Looking as tall as possible and expanding the chest is universally employed by human beings as a means of intimidating an adversary. The exaggerated wide-shoulder cut of business suit jackets and some uniforms are designed to give the appearance of power.

Like it or not, the size of a man's chest has a powerful sexual effect on females. And it is usually a case of "the larger the better." Men also stand with their hands akimbo, on their hips, which widens, expands and visually enlarges the chest, making the man look more powerful than he may actually be.

The throat dimple, below the Adam's apple, is very vulnerable and suggests openness and submission if put on display. The human neck is rather slim in both men and women so men may "widen" their necks with buttoned-up shirts and knotted ties. A long tie adds an eye-catching line to accent the vertically ascending height of the face, head and torso and the shirt-collar points juxtapose to form a visual arrow shape, which points upward and thereby draws eyes to the man's face.

The female breast is probably the single largest sexual preoccupation among men. This connects directly to the infant experience of breastfeeding. It is an entirely predictable if somewhat disheartening fact: men love breasts. Everything about breasts is comforting and arousing for men in equal measure. Pert breasts and especially erect nipples are guaranteed under almost any circumstances to become objects of fixation to men. Unfortunately this obsession causes many women to become anxious about their own breasts and has spawned a depressingly large plastic surgery industry.

When women are aroused in a public setting they often stroke their necks as an alternative to actually stroking their breasts. Jewelry, especially a pendant, acts as a pointer, drawing attention to the tantalizing cleavage below.

The sexy torso

Looking comfortable in our body is central to appearing attractive to others.

The stomach

This area is particularly significant considering that, of all the muscles that affect male sexual performance during coitus, it is the stomach muscles that matter most. In order to be fit for fine and long-lasting love-making, strengthen your stomach muscles. It is also a strong signifier in both sexes of youth and its associated fertility. In many cultures the display of the female bare stomach is considered highly sexual yet still respectable.

The back

Our backs are beautiful, but we sometimes forget all about them. The dictates of fashion mean that women have a considerable advantage over men here. An expanse of back, or even glimpses of it through translucent material or peek-a-boo gaps in the cloth, send a fabulous sexual signal.

The shoulders are eminently capable of flashing sexual signals. A shoulder revealed, stroked or shrugged can be deliciously provocative. The curves and roundness of shoulders, particularly in women, are sensuous and arousing.

The entire length of your spine is exquisitely erotic, from the tiny hairs at the nape of the neck to the supersensitive dimples at the base of the spine just above your buttocks.

A glimpse of a flat stomach is highly arousing for both sexes, but especially for men when displayed by women.

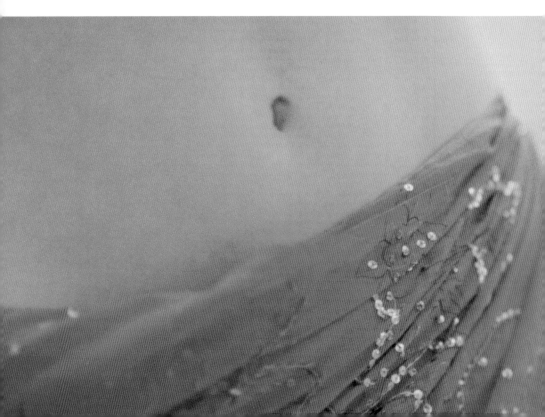

Posture and movements

Someone with a generally well-balanced, upright posture really stands out as special and attractive. Such a person has presence, and will be described as elegant, distinguished and beautiful.

Many of us misuse our bodies a lot of the time. We slouch, we slump, we let ourselves become unfit. We sit in chairs apparently designed to distort our backs, crouch for hours in front of computer screens, and so on. Our physical posture can both reflect and partly dictate our moods. When we are miserable, we droop, and when we droop, we are miserable. When we are feeling positive our posture tends to be positive and, by the same token, a confident posture tends to make us feel good and other people will perceive us as sexy.

1

1 People tend to stand and walk with a slack stomach and hunched shoulders: their backs are crooked and their hips lopsided.

2 As a man and woman come within close visual range they both pull in their stomachs, throw their shoulders back, puff up their chests, lift up their heads to appear taller and generally attempt to make themselves appear sleeker and more youthful.

Attention!

Research shows that when two people of the opposite sex come into close enough proximity to feel aroused and mutually attracted, a number of significant physical changes take place.

Changes in posture and movement are easiest to spot in public places where little clothing is worn – for example, at a swimming pool or on the beach. Muscle tone tightens, skin texture changes, blood flows to our faces, necks and sometimes our genitals. Our breathing rate increases, our palms sweat and we experience all the physiological symptoms associated with adrenaline release.

Dance

In most cultures of the world, both music and dance are central components of courtship rituals.

To be a skilled lover requires some degree of talent for rhythm. It is something we look for in prospective partners, and we can see it most obviously in the way a person moves their body in response to a beat.

Dancing provides great opportunities for sexual signalling: armpits can be flashed, with the hands raised in the air or touching the hair, providing a provocative sensual signal. The same is true of rolling shoulders and running one's hands over one's body. These apply equally to men and women.

Dancing is a dramatic way to put on a preening display for prospective mates and it is an acceptable way of showing off our talents. Many dance movements involve swaying the hips and torso and the stylized mimicking of sexual acts. The way we dance reflects our mood, shows how vividly we respond to music and gives onlookers strong clues about our personality. Our body movements will certainly show if we like the music we are dancing to. Dancing also provides great opportunities for mirroring and postural echoing.

Men and women exhibit certain stereotyped behaviors while dancing. The women dance in a group together, sometimes forming a circle, which apparently excludes men. Men gather in groups at the edge of the dance floor, or prowl around in packs like wolves on the hunt. If the men dance it is normally in pairs or alone, and they take their cue from the dance floor, when they notice single girls dancing outside the female circle.

People not dancing but wanting to do so will indicate this with their bodies. Although they may be talking to others, they will move their hands or feet gently to the rhythm of the music, or sway their upper torso and shoulders in small dance movements. If you are interested in asking someone to dance, wait to see these "I wish I were dancing" body signals before moving in. The more obvious the movements the more likely it is that a person will accept.

The slow dance is often the first opportunity we have to become really intimate with someone. Check out the responses while you are dancing – where our arms are; how we move our bodies; how close together we bring our upper torsos; how much we allow our leg or knee to project between the legs of the other person; how tightly we hold each other; how much we relax into each other's arms; the amount of time we spend looking into each other's eyes; whether our partner is looking over our shoulder or resisting our attempts to move his or her face into position so that kissing is possible – all these tell us everything we need to know about our levels of sexual readiness.

A full-torso-to-full-torso position is quite hostile unless we are dancing, which not only allows us to adopt this pose within social conventions but also ensures that any confrontational stance is not maintained for long – the end of a particular song provides a convenient opportunity to withdraw gracefully from any further intimacy with no excuses needed.

Hips and butts

Anatomical differences are responsible for the characteristic ways in which men and women walk. In women there is a greater rolling action of the pelvis, which causes more swinging of the hips.

Swinging hips

The hip-swinging walk can send a powerful sexual signal. The way a woman walks across a room can mean the difference between attracting a great deal of attention and being totally ignored. Length of leg is another arousal signal. Actual length is not as important as relative length: this is why slender legs are considered more aesthetically pleasing, as they appear to be longer. High heels increase leg length and are consequently considered sexy.

The hip thrust combined with the placing of her hand on her hip exaggerates the feminine hourglass figure.

Sexy buttocks

Female curves can be emphasized by placing a hand on one or both hips and placing the body weight on one leg, while turning your torso at an angle to the man desired.

Women's buttocks are a strong source of sexual signals for men because the rear-entry position is still ingrained in the male psyche as the natural position for sex. Clothes that either hint at, or actually show the shape of, a woman's rear send shock waves of arousal through men. When a woman places her hand in the back pocket of a tight-fitting pair of jeans the rounded shape of the buttocks is emphasized still further. Rubbing a hand over the outline has much the same effect.

The more rounded and pert a woman's buttocks are, the stronger the sexual signal becomes. The emphasis that so many clothes give to the breast cleavage is intended to suggest the image of swollen buttocks often associated with mating behavior.

But women don't miss out: many visually assess the buttocks of men whenever the opportunity to do so presents itself. A small, tightly muscled behind is considered particularly sexy by most Western women.

Few men can resist admiring a woman who walks by with swinging hips and a confident "look-at-me" energy.

Legs and feet

The legs and feet have their own sexual language, and are particularly involved in the blocking and territory-marking aspects of seduction.

Many people think that crossing the legs is a defensive signal or a way of repressing sexuality. Sometimes this may be the case, but legs that cross can send many other signals too.

The standard leg-cross, where the right leg is rested over the left in a relaxed manner, can be used as a protective or closed position, depending on the context. A protective stance is adopted when the leg-crosser feels threatened – the crotch area is hidden behind the shield of the upper thighs pressed together.

If legs are crossed defensively this will usually be accompanied by a range of other defensive signals – the arms may be folded, eye contact will be furtive, not flirtatious. If a woman is feeling very uncomfortable, she may even have her handbag in her lap as a substitute fig-leaf and will lean her torso away from the offending person, or lean forwards with her head supported by one arm which she is using to shield herself.

Crossed legs can be used as a form of pointing and send out a vital signal. When sitting, we tend to cross our legs towards the person we are attracted to, and away from someone to whom we wish to send a negative sexual signal. We can point a crossed leg directly at someone we like, or in their general direction. We also point with our feet and especially the toes.

When standing, we point a foot towards someone who attracts us, or move a leg towards them. We can shift our weight onto the back leg with the other leg forwards and bent at the knee. The female knee has a particularly erotic effect on some men, its roundness hinting at the shape of breast and buttock.

We can point with our knees too, and if we really stretch a leg towards someone we can use it as an invitation to follow it back to where it begins. Men tend to use the standard leg-cross through habit or simply because they sit in a bad posture.

Both men and women sometimes cross their legs at the ankle, and the message this gives should be interpreted in the context of accompanying signals – particularly how widely apart the legs are spread.

Long slim legs are equally appealing in both men and women. A short skirt will always attract the attention of men, while skirts with slits that partly reveal legs are often perceived as more alluring. Here the man receives positive foot and knee points.

The crotch display

Legs parted in a great yawning splay send a crude primitive sexual signal. Nevertheless, both men and women do automatically open their legs to varying degrees when in the presence of someone they find particularly attractive. It is more common for men to sit with their legs open, often giving a crotch display, though women wearing trousers do this too. Tight-fitting trousers are highly provocative if they outline the shape of the female genitals through the material as well as emphasizing the curves of the bottom.

The "open 4"

The cross-legged position known as "open 4," with one ankle placed on top of the other knee, can be very inviting when used by either men or women, but if they are blocking the crossed leg with one hand, this is a more defensive signal.

Sitting with legs slightly apart sends a message of openness and approachability. It sends a cue to men that she is interested in potential suitors attempting to impress her.

Playing footsie

Playing footsie is usually, but not always, reserved for people already in a relationship.

It can be very exciting, especially if it occurs out of sight (under a table, for instance) and especially if it is performed secretively in the presence of others. What dinner-table entertainment could be more arousing than to have your partner (or perhaps a new acquaintance with whom you have been exchanging signals of mutual attraction) touch your feet, ankles or lower leg furtively while above the table he or she remains apparently deep in conversation with someone else?

As flirting intensifies, we often accidentally touch each other. A foot brushing against a shin is overtly sexual but can be excused as a mistake if it is not received well.

Using all the senses

If the two of you are to become intimate, all your other senses will be of great importance. Slow down and luxuriate with your partner, enjoy the sensation of skin-on-skin touch. Two people in love who are really connected to each other can hold entire conversations without murmuring a word.

Using your voice

It's not what you say but the way that you say it! Try the following revealing experiment.

Try saying to yourself,"Oh darling, I love you." Now try saying it aloud. Now say it in a heavy French accent. Now with a funny croaky voice. Now with your tongue pressed into your cheek. Now say it really slowly, making the "Oh" last a long time. Say it really breathily this time. Now put the emphasis on "I." Then shift the emphasis to "you." Say it as if you were frightened. Say it loudly. Say it hurriedly. Then be very quiet and say it as you do when you really do love someone. You will see that musical tonality is more attractive than a voice that adheres to a monotone.

On the telephone

After a first meeting which has gone well you will probably have exchanged telephone numbers, though one of you may have withheld their number. Social norms differ, but in the West most men ask for a girl's number first. If you've got business cards, you might swap these as well. If both numbers are exchanged then the man is generally expected to make the first contact. Whatever the circumstances of obtaining the number, the first telephone call is usually invigorating and even nerve wracking. Telephones hide most of the subtleties of our voices so you must rely utterly on the tiniest variation of tone and speed that can be detected. However, moods can be guessed at quite accurately just from the sound of a voice.

Doubts and hesitations are as obvious as the sound of someone smiling as they talk to you. Given this, the best way to make a telephone call is to imagine that the person you are calling is in the room with you, that he or she can see you, so that you take conscious note of your body language and adjust it accordingly. Flirt with your prospective date by sending them attractive and inviting body signals, even though they're not actually present.

The digital age

A multitude of new possibilities in sexual communication has arrived with the digital age. Declarations of love have been imparted in written form since the ancients, but the new generation of instant and often abbreviated or coded messages requires special consideration. People tend to be bolder when they write than when they speak.

The immediate absence of the other person seems to provide the writer with a lower level of inhibition. As a consequence millions of highly charged flirtatious and sexual messages are exchanged daily the world over. More relationships have also come unglued as a consequence of the discovery or wrong-sending of erotic exchanges.

Chat rooms, instant messaging and even e-mails also provide plenty of opportunity for people to express themselves more openly than they might feel capable of in the direct presence of others. But be cautious – the written word cannot be withdrawn as easily as a spoken indiscretion. And the power of the written word should not be underestimated.

On-line dating is big business as is cell phone picture dating – agencies are springing up all over the world. This strange random and instantaneous access to potential partners requires us to be starkly aware of the importance of first impressions. The image or video clip you present of yourself is going to give strangers the opportunity to make important judgements about you in seconds. Look and sound your best. If you appear vital, joyful and healthy you will significantly increase your attraction levels. Presenting the body language of confidence, self-assurance and flirtatiousness will all increase the likelihood of romantic possibilities.

Imagine that the person you are talking to is in the room with you, observing all the positive body-language signals you are communicating.

Scent

All of us stink! We all smell too! Signals from the nose are interpreted by the brain in the olfactory bulb, located in that part of the brain that is assigned to memory and other higher-thinking processes.

Our natural smell is unique. Each one of us has a particular odor produced by a complex combination of our skin texture and the sebaceous glands under the surface of the skin that secrete various oily deposits. How we smell varies depending on the level of different chemicals in our bodies, and on the natural sugars, acids, alkaline and salts that are deposited on the skin's surface and released from glands located in the groin, armpits, mouth, eyelids, nipples and, to a lesser degree, the backs of the knees, the wrists and from the palms of the hands.

It is this personal smell that carries a great deal of important information to the olfactory center of a potential lover. If the body smell is not right, there will almost certainly be no attraction. We therefore do ourselves a disservice by applying too many products that cover up our olfactory identity. So why do we do it? The answer is simple. Our clothes trap and hold the natural scents – pheromones – that are released from the various sites around our body (which are usually hair-covered since the hairs help distribute the scents into the air around us), causing them to become stale and unpleasant, so we mask them with artificial perfumes.

Enhancing sex appeal

Do perfumes and deodorants, body creams and oils, and the many washing agents and conditioners we use on our clothes actually enhance our sexual appeal?

From the vast amounts of money that are spent upon them you would think the answer must be yes, but it is not that clear. Smells are capable of eliciting particularly strong memories. Obviously, a memory-related attraction prompted by a particular smell, such as being temporarily attracted to someone because they wear the same aftershave as an ex-lover, is only a rare event. However, when we buy perfumes for our lovers, are we saying to them, "I wish you smelled like someone I loved before" or, worse still, "I don't like your natural smell, so I'd like you to cover it with this, please"?

The smell of sex

Research shows that our body smells change as we become turned on, and that the scents given off even change during love-making as we approach orgasm. The pheromones in men and women are different. The male pheromone, called androsterone, is related to the male sex hormone testosterone, which is produced in the testes. Perfume-makers add a chemically similar substance called andostenediol to various perfumes for men with the specific intent of increasing sexual attraction.

Androsterone is especially evident in the armpits and groin. Thus a man who is clean but not covered with a perfume, and who has not blocked up the pores of his skin with a deodorant, is most likely to sexually arouse women. This may be why men often sit with their legs open when they are trying to seduce. It is not just that they wish to show their suggestive crotch bulge – they also unconsciously want their natural scent to waft into the air.

Women's pheromones, called capulins, are released in the sweat glands and also vaginal secretions. The rules about cleanliness apply to women in the same way as they do to men. Women are often able to identify a perfume that seems to exaggerate their natural smell. A little perfume goes a very long way: if you can smell it on yourself you've probably got too much on. Some natural scents have long been associated with sexual arousal – for example, ambergris, civet, musk, vanilla and violets.

It takes courage, but one way to turn on a person by smell is to unbutton your shirt, rub your hand under your armpit, then wipe your face and neck with it! However, this is not a technique that you should try out on a stranger.

Our sense of smell is vital during intimate sexual encounters. By luxuriating in each other's natural scents we significantly deepen our connection to them, partly because smells are so connected to our emotional responses.

Touch

Every inch of your body is sensitive to touch. Self-touch for
public display purposes is known as preening, and this is an
integral part of courtship behavior.

Preening is a way of flattering ourselves and flirting with others simultaneously.
It occurs throughout the animal kingdom, usually with the males of the species
parading to impress potential mates. Both men and women preen themselves
alone, often as part of the ritual of dressing to go out. Once in the presence of
the opposite sex, they begin to preen again. The most common preening
gestures are touching the hair with hands, comb or brush; touching the face
(normally with fingertips) in brief stroking gestures, including wiping the
eyebrows, touching the lips or ears, stroking the cheeks, and smoothing the
beard or moustache.

    If we want to send non-verbal sexual signals to another person we put
on a display by preening towards them, flicking our hair back from our face,
for example, and running a hand through it while simultaneously casting a
glance towards our target. We brush imaginary fluff from our shoulders, pick
at invisible specks of dust and endlessly rearrange our whole attire.

    If the clothes we are wearing are made from fine, sensuous materials,
especially silks, suede and fine cottons, we may be aroused by the sensation
of them against our skin. Women tend to stroke their breasts – especially the
upper part of the breast – with a finger or with unconscious strokes of the
hand. This touching may cause their nipples to become firm and erect.
Although erect nipples can also be the result of temperature change or just
friction against material and need not be related in any way to sexual arousal,
the non-verbal signal sent is sensational. Men tend to be unable to look
anywhere else if they notice a woman's erect nipples beneath clothing.

    Auto-erotic signalling, as this self-touch display and preening behavior
is called, is a precursor to the touch of another person. We are preparing
ourselves mentally and physically for a possible sexual encounter. Once we
are ready, we demonstrate our readiness.

Private preparation rituals and public preening displays are observed in both men and women during all stages of a developing relationship. When we are attracted to someone we unconsciously fuss over our appearance, as if readjusting our breeding plumage. We tug on cuffs, readjust ties, scarves and clothes, brush away imaginary fluff from our clothes, check make-up, smooth our eyebrows and touch and stroke our hair.

Early touch in courtship

To invite touch is to make yourself accessible and vulnerable. This takes trust and courage and suggests that attraction is growing between you.

We have all experienced the inevitable anxieties of potential rejection. It is a nerve-racking thing to ask another person for a first date, or for a dance, or even just to strike up a conversation with them. To offer someone a hand literally, or metaphorically, and have it refused can be a substantial blow to the ego. The successful use of touch, therefore, depends on good timing and the accurate reading of the other person's non-verbal sexual signals.

How and when you first touch obviously depends on your situation. If you are going to rush across a busy road together you may instinctively join hands as you step off the curb. If you are walking along side by side, you may offer your hand passively and find it being held. You may suddenly want to point out something in a shop window and grab your companion enthusiastically. Alternatively, you may guide him or her with a gentle hand on the lower back.

Parties are ideal venues for first physical contact, allowing people to touch by dancing together. The simple act of passing any object to a person presents you with the chance to touch or be touched, whether you are handing over a pen, or a glass of wine, or passing them their coat.

The importance of developing touching skills cannot be overestimated. Men are particularly prone to being insensitive, rushed and rough in their touch. Becoming mindful of the power of very gentle touching always enhances attraction.

Playing with food is a common precursor to love-making. Allowing ourselves to be fed suggests submission and trust. It also has erotic connotations because of the oral delight involved.

Mutual grooming

A sincere sign of attraction is to preen or groom someone else. This can be done without putting on pressure or suggesting you are making assumptions about the progress of the relationship. To pluck a piece of fluff from another's lapel is completely innocuous yet bodes well for intimacy.

When you engage in non-verbal dialogue, keep reading their signs for invitations or acceptance of touch. If you do touch, check your own responses and theirs. If you both feel comfortable and "right," then continue. If the other person withdraws or tenses up, or if the non-verbal signals change abruptly, respond by releasing your hold on them and by giving them some space. Keep your body language warm and positive but be aware of how much personal space your opposite number needs in order to feel safe. What you want to avoid is the negative cascade of awkward feelings and misunderstandings.

Good manners combine the opportunity to be gallant with the possibility of ritualized grooming. A person's response to non-sexual touch will usually indicate their pleasure or discomfort at the contact.

Touching each other

Here is a list of the usual sequence of touching escalation:

- Hand to hand
- Hand to forearm
- Linked arms
- Hand to shoulder
- Arm around waist
- Hand to hair/head
- Lips to lips
- Hand to neck, back, knees, breasts, thighs
- Deep kissing
- Hand to genitals (still clothed)
- Mouth to breast/chest
- Mouth to whole body
- Hands remove each other's clothes
- Full love-making

Physical intimacy develops in predictable stages of intensity. Women complain, rightly, that men often rush the natural progression from non-sexual to full sexual touch. By paying careful attention to the signals from a lover, we can read the speed at which they desire us to proceed.

Loving touch

With increased confidence and knowledge and the practical application of your non-verbal sexual skills, you will feel really good giving and receiving, offering and asking for quality touch with your lover.

Touch between two people changes everything; wherever two bodies touch, both of them are connected to each other physically, taking the dynamic between those two people on to a whole new dimension of interaction.

Sensitivity to the timing of touch can mean the difference between increased intimacy or, alternatively, withdrawal and rejection. Tune in to the signals that your partner's body and your own are sending, and act upon them thoughtfully. In the times when one of you is feeling a need for more space you should be sensitive to, and understanding of, this need. It does not mean you are being rejected – it is simply that each of us has times when we feel like withdrawing and isolating ourselves from a lover. Use your touch to reassure, and remember that when the person close to you needs extra room to breathe, you should allow them the space, just as you would want them to do for you.

The whole picture

This section presents you with the chance to test your own skills at reading other people's sexual signals of attraction and explains how to interpret the often complex and sometimes contradictory signals that people display.

The Rule of Four

The Lloyd-Elliott Rule of Four states that,"To be sure that another person is communicating unequivocal non-verbal sexual interest in you, he or she must be displaying a minimum of four separate positive signals simultaneously, and these signals must be directed at you."

A person who is sexually aroused may display some positive signals unconsciously, independent of other people present. Do not assume that the person displaying four signals is necessarily directing them at you. You also need to bear in mind that one of the complex games that people play is to flirt with everyone except the person in whom they are really interested. You may fall victim to being used as a pawn in an intrigue-filled chess game.

Remember, too, that moods, feelings and physical levels of arousal can all change quickly. Someone may come on to you strongly with four sexual signals, but the moment you actually start talking to them, they may change their minds and their body language. Keep your eyes working in conjunction with your brain. If you start to receive negative signals, such as a drop in attentiveness and a general reduction in rapport, there is no need to make a fool of yourself, or to make someone else feel awkward – just back off with grace. Psychologists call these non-verbal negative signals de-courting signals.

Do remember that one positive signal can lead to two, three or ten signals in five minutes, an hour or even three months. There is no limit to the length of time that may elapse between the first minutes of meeting and eventual commitment to some form of relationship. Many signals of attraction may be seen in people who are just friends. Indeed, some of the best sexual relationships develop from friendships. Test yourself. Imagine you are observing a person of the opposite sex and that he or she is aware that you are watching. How many different signals can you read?

If the person in question is leaning towards you and smiling, but scanning the room for someone else, they are probably being friendly while waiting for their date. If their arms are folded but you are getting wonderful eye contact, genuine smiles and a leg and foot are being pointed at you, try handing over a drink to see if they open their body up to you. If you notice face touches, hair preening and sideways glances, but the person has their legs crossed away from you and is hand in hand with someone else, they may be flirting with you even though they seem committed. On the other hand, if your non-verbal conversation skills serve you well, the commitment might be broken and they may turn their attention to you.

There are at least ten separate positive signals, one ambiguous and one negative signal being displayed among this group. Attraction reveals itself in the repeated and varied positive signals being displayed.

1 The open palm is a positive warm gesture. The hands point towards the object of their desire.

2 Mirroring happens when two people begin to unconsciously synchronize their movements.

3 The head tilt, especially combined with exposing the neck, is a sign of submission and invites approach from potential suitors.

4 Self-touching occurs when we are in the company of someone we find very attractive. We signal our unconscious desire to touch the other person or to have them touch us.

5 The wrist display is very alluring and indicates positive feelings of attraction are being experienced. The wrists are so vulnerable they accentuate the feminine. They are important enough in seduction to be a key place for applying perfume too.

6 Ambiguous signals include crossed arms, and tension in the hands and fingers. Fingers pressing tight into the upper arm suggest anxiety or shyness. This is an example of non-verbal leakage, as she is probably trying to keep her fear hidden.

7 Her leg and knee point respond positively to his cowboy crotch point. Also her foot slipping in and out of her shoe indicates strong arousal. This gesture often happens outside of people's awareness as we focus least on our hands and feet.

8 When a man stands in the classic cowboy stance, he is feeling sexy, confident and dominant. If a man stands like this while facing a particular woman, it is certain that he finds her highly attractive and wishes to impress her with his strength and potency.

Conflicting signals

As with so many other areas of human behavior, we are confronted daily with contradiction and inconsistency in non-verbal communication.

It is a general feature that with humans few things are ever clear-cut. We are complex creatures who operate on many levels; a woman may be very attracted to a man at first glance but may quash her natural inclinations and desires as she remembers that she is already committed elsewhere. Alternatively, she may remember the pain of ending a previous relationship, or a friend's warning about this man.

Conflicting internal and external messages create the uncomfortable condition of simultaneous attraction towards and repulsion from the potential source of attraction or hurt. And while the intellectual argument rages, internally the woman's body may be providing her with a complicated chemistry of physical desire. A man is just as likely to undergo similar internal conflicts. Sometimes people find themselves in the dilemma of thinking they don't find someone attractive while simultaneously being inexorably drawn towards them. This will inevitably be communicated non-verbally, leading to conflicting messages. Bear in mind, however, that with time thoughts and feelings can change.

Her arms being crossed and her leg crossed away from him suggest she is defended and not attracted by his advances. But her warm sincere smile and face alignment send the opposite signals. She may be experiencing conflicting emotions that show in her body language.

1 Open palms, direct eye contact and a sincere symmetrical smile indicate that the truth is being told.

2 The shrug of the shoulders, combined with a look of exasperation at not being believed and the turning in of the fingers suggest that he may be lying.

3 His open left palm is vulnerable and appealing, yet he is rubbing his face. Perhaps he is not telling the whole truth.

4 We touch our noses or mouth when lying. Yet his eye contact and facial expression suggest he is honest. More visual clues are required before we can be sure of the whole truth.

Lies and deception

People often ask psychologists if they can read what people are thinking just by observing their body language and, in particular, whether they can tell if someone is lying.

We are brought up to think that lying is bad. Most of us are encouraged to develop a keen sense of right and wrong and to feel guilty if we avoid telling the truth. As a result, as with any strong emotion, conflicts that occur inside us tend to leak out, showing themselves in our non-verbal behavior. The extent to which this leakage shows itself when we lie is often related to the possible consequences of discovery, or to the seriousness of deception. The "white lie," in which we excuse ourselves on the grounds that a lie is for the best, allows us to evade feeling guilty, and so is difficult to detect.

  None of the following non-verbal signals are in themselves actual proof of deception. All of them can be caused by other psychological states or physical pressures, but they do tend to be associated with deception and if two or more of them occur simultaneously you should take it into consideration that a person may be lying to you. Assuming that people are scared as they lie (which is a big assumption), their automatic nervous system will cause the following:

* Heavier sweating, particularly in the palms, which may become itchy
* Uneven breathing
* Dry throat and lips becoming dry, accompanied by swallowing more frequently
* Slower speech, but with more slips of the tongue
* Blushing
* Leakage such as twiddling of pens, doodling
* Avoidance of physical contact.

The inner conflict that takes place when we lie prompts a series of subtle but perceivable twitches, micro gestures and facial movements that flash across the face in under a second. We notice these gestures, though we are often not consciously aware that we have done so. People who are lying often exhibit minute nervous tics in the muscles of their mouths, usually only on one side, and in their cheeks or eyelids. They may also blink faster, their eyebrows may twitch – again usually on one side – and their shoulders may move slightly.

1 Although her open palms suggest that [sh]e is truthful, her [a]wkward body posture [an]d strained expression [im]ply an inner tension [th]at may be caused by [di]shonesty.

2 Some people close their eyes as they [li]e in order to prevent the [li]stener from seeing [d]eception in the "windows [to] the soul." A lopsided [s]mile often gives away [in]sincerity as well.

Of course, a still photograph does not give the whole picture, as it is movement that betrays a lie. Someone who is lying will often fidget, drum the fingertips or entwine the fingers together. Toes will flex inside shoes, and the feet, especially if they are hidden from view, may tap agitatedly.

Most importantly, we almost always seem to revert to the childhood habit of taking our hands to our mouths as soon as a lie is spoken. The response is similar to that of a child revealing a big secret, realizing that he has blundered, then grasping at the invisible words as if they were still floating in the air, capable of being stuffed back into the offending orifice from which they have so recently sprung.

As we develop a more sophisticated control over the body language that landed us in trouble when we were children, we still respond to lying with the automatic mouth clamp, but the action is slowed. This slowing allows our brain to interrupt the natural process, overriding it by diverting our hands to a site nearby – most often the edge of the mouth, the nose (especially the underside), the cheek or the chin. This delay may range from a couple of seconds to as much as a minute. People sometimes wipe the mouth with a downward open-palm gesture, as if to clean away guilt induced by their uncomfortable conscience.

Is honesty therefore always a better option? Well, yes, in that you will probably be caught out by the person you are lying to anyway – although they may choose not to let on or even to acknowledge this insight to themselves – but on the other hand maybe no, as the social conventions of politeness, flirtation and flattery sometimes oblige us to compliment or deceive in order to boost confidence or avoid obvious insult. If your date asks you if you like his suit you would do better to not tell him you think it stinks, especially if you know that he has gone to a lot of trouble to look nice for you. (However, if he asks you if he has bad breath you will be doing both of you a favor if you tell him the truth!)

Do remember that one positive signal can lead to two, three or ten signals in five minutes, an hour or even three months. There is no limit to the length of time that may elapse between the first minutes of meeting and eventual commitment to some form of relationship.

3 In adults, touching the mouth can indicate anxiety, particularly in relation to recent or imminent speech.

4 Her relaxed stance, natural, balanced smile and open body posture all suggest that she is telling him the truth.

Time to talk

There comes a point where verbal communication must begin if an encounter is to move on to the next step.

If you are unsure about the signals you have been receiving, now is the time to check them out. Verbal and non-verbal dialogue interact and all the non-verbal sexual signals identified so far continue after verbal dialogue has begun.

When a person's verbal language contradicts what their body language is saying, give greater weight to the latter. If someone tells you that they are "not interested" in a teasing and flirtatious way but continues to send you very sexual signals, they may just be playing hard to get or saying "chase me." But if someone clearly means "no, leave me alone," you must respect this. Persistence in the face of rejection seldom brings about a positive outcome.

Remind yourself to read the whole picture, not just a part of it. The human body speaks from head to toe. It is your task to gather up all the different pieces of the jigsaw puzzle and play the detective so that you can assemble it correctly. It is unwise to focus on one or two very positive non-verbal signals while overlooking many other accompanying negative ones. The combined message may be profoundly and often disappointingly different from its individual components.

Conclusion

We instinctively accept the old adage that like attracts like, in some respects at least. We want people to like the same things as we do because mutuality and compatibility make us feel that we are less likely to be rejected and more likely to be loved for ourselves. Similarity breeds content, but opposites attract. Both contradictory statements are true: there are almost as many celebrated couples who look alike physically as there are apparent mismatches, for example, between very tall, beautiful women and short, dumpy men.

What matters is this: do not limit yourself by buying into the myth that you have to be very attractive physically in order to have romantic success in life. The desire for instant gratification of lust may rely on the superficial "red flag" of the model Adonis or Aphrodite, but like any false god's promise, the pleasure is always temporary, and is followed by a feeling of emptiness or regret, and a longing for something of more depth. The real riches of any relationship are not the static ones of looks and physique but the ongoing "dynamic" ones of vitality, communication, conversation, tactics, compatability, touch, intimacy and, of course, body language.

As we fall in love, our faces begin to glow, the bags under our eyes decrease, we frown less, we smile more, our skin blooms and we can look younger, our eyes have a certain dreamy glaze, and our general expression changes so markedly that other people remark upon it.

Bibliography

Alicke, M. D., Smith, R.H., & Klotz. "Judgements of physical attractiveness; the role of faces and bodies." *Personality and Social Psychology* Bulletin 12 (1986), 381-9.

Ardrey, R. *The Territorial Imperative*. Collins, London, 1967.

Argyle, M. *Bodily Communication*. 2nd edition, Methuen, London, 1988.

Argyle, M. *Social Interaction*. Methuen, London, 1968.

Argyle, M. *The Psychology of Interpersonal Behaviour*. Penguin Books, 1967.

Argyle, M., Furnham, A. & Graham, E. J .A. *Social Situations*. Cambridge University Press, 1981.

Argyle, M. & Henderson, M. *The Anatomy of Friendships*. Penguin Books, 1985.

Aronson, E. *The Social Animal*. 2nd edition, Freeman, San Francisco, 1976.

Axtell, R. E. *Gestures*. Wiley, New York, 1991.

Berscheid, E. "Interpersonal Attraction," in *Handbook of Social Psychology*, edited by G. Lindzey & E. Aronson. Random House, New York, 1985.

Bettleheim, B. *The Uses of Enchantment*. Knopf, New York, 1976.

Birwhistell, R. L. *Introduction to Kinesics*. University of Louisville Press, 1952.

Birwhistell, R. L. *Kinesics and Context*. Allen Lane, London, 1971.

Brownmiller, S. *Femininity*. Paladin, London, 1986.

Brun, T. *The International Dictionary of Sign Language*. Wolfe, London, 1969.

Cahoon, D. D. & Edmonds, E. M. "Male-female estimates of opposite sex first impressions concerning females' clothing styles." *Bulletin of the Psychonomic Society* 27 (1989), 280-1.

Carnegie, D. *How to Win Friends and Influence People*. Angus & Robertson, Sydney, 1965.

Cohen, D. *Body Language in Relationships*. Sheldon Press, London, 1992.

Colton, H. *The Gift of Touch*. Putnam's, New York, 1983

Cook, M. & Wilson, G. (eds). *Love and Attraction*. Pergamon Press, Oxford, 1979.

Critchley, M. *Silent Language*. Butterworth, London, 1975.

Dale-Guthrie, R. *Body Hot-Spots*. Van Nostrand Rheinhold, New York, 1976.

Danziger, K. *Interpersonal Communication*. Pergamon Press, Oxford, 1976.

Davitz, J. R. *The Communication of Emotional Meaning*. McGraw-Hill, New York, 1964.

Dodson, B. *Sex for One*. Harmony Books, 1987.

Duck, S. *Human Relationships*. 2nd edition, Sage, London, 1992.

Ekman, P. *Darwin and Facial Expression*. Academic Press, New York, 1973.

Ekman, P. & Friesen, W. *Unmasking the Face*. Prentice Hall, London, 1975.

Ekman, P. *Telling Lies*. Norton, 1985.

Fast, J. *Body Language*. Pan, London, 1970.

Gahagan, J. *Social Interaction and Its Management*. Methuen, London, 1984.

Givens, D. *Love Signals*. Crown, New York, 1983.

Goffman, E. *Interaction Ritual*. Allen Lane, London, 1972.

Goldman, W. & Lewis, P. "Beautiful is good: evidence that the physically attractive are more socially skilful." *Journal of Experimental Social Psychology* 13 (1977), 125-30.

Hall, E. T. *Silent Language*. Doubleday & Co., New York, 1959.

Hall, E. T. *The Hidden Dimension*. New York, 1966.

Hargreaves, D. J. & Colley, A. M. (eds). *The Psychology of Sex Roles*. Harper & Row, New York, 1986.

Hartley, P. *Interpersonal Communication*. Routledge, London, 1993.

Henley, N. M. *Body Politics: Power, Sex and Non-verbal Communication*. Prentice-Hall, 1977.

Hess, E. H. "Pupilometrics" in *Handbook of Psychophysiology*, edited by N. Greenfield & R. Sternbach. Holt, Reinhart & Winston, New York, 1972.

Hinde, R. A. (ed). *Nonverbal Communication*. Cambridge University Press, 1972.

Hinton, P. R. *The Psychology of Interpersonal Perception*. Routledge, London, 1993.

Hopkins, C. *Man Hunting*. Angus & Robertson, 1990.

Hopkins, C. *Girl Chasing*. Angus & Robertson, 1991.

Huston, T. C. "Ambiguity of Acceptance, Social Desirability, and Dating Choice." *Journal of Experimental Social Psychology* 9 (1973), 32-42.

Kahn, E. J. & Rudnitsky, D. *Love Codes*. Signet, 1992.

Kalick, S. M. "Physical attractiveness as a status cue." *Journal of Experimental Social Psychology* 24 (1988) 469-89.

Key, M. R. *Non-verbal communication: A Research Guide and Bibliography*. Scarecrow Press, New Jersey, 1977.

Kleinke, C. L. "Gaze and eye contact; a research review." *Psychological Bulletin* 100 (1986), 78-100.

Kurtz, R., & Prestera, H. *The Body Reveals*. Harper & Row, New York, 1984.

Lamb, W. *Body Code*. Routledge & Kegan Paul, London, 1979.

Lewis, D. *The Secret Language of Success*. Bantam Press, London, 1989.

Liggett, J. *The Human Face*. Constable, London, 1974.

Lont, C. M. & Friedley, S. A. (eds). *Beyond Boundaries: Sex and Gender Diversity in Communication*. George Mason University Press, 1989.

Lyle, J. *Body Language*. Hamlyn, London, 1991.

Maslow, A. H. *The Farther Reaches of Human Behaviour*. Viking Press, New York, 1971.

Masters, W. H. & Johnson, V. E. *Human Sexual Response*. Little, Brown, Boston, 1966.

Morris, D. *Intimate Behaviour*. Jonathan Cape, London, 1971.

Morris, D. *Manwatching*. Jonathan Cape, 1977.

Mortimer, J. (ed). *Great Law and Order Stories*. Penguin Books, London, 1990.

Pease, A. *Body Language*. Sheldon Press, London, 1984.

Poyatos, F. *New Perspectives in Nonverbal Communication*. Sage, London, 1983.

Quilliam, S. *Sexual Body Talk*. Headline, London, 1993.

Sigall, H. & Landy, D. "Radiating beauty: effects of having a physically attractive partner on person perception." *Journal of Personality and Social Psychology* 28 (1973), 218-24.

Simpson, J. A., Gangestad, S. W. & Lenna, M. "Perception of physical attractiveness: mechanisms involved in the maintenance of romantic relationships." *Journal of Personality and Social Psychology* 59 (1990), 1192-1201.

Smith, M. J. *When I Say No I Feel Guilty*. Bantam, 1975.

Symons, D. *The Evolution of Human Sexuality*. Oxford University Press, 1979.

Wainwright, G. R. *Body Language*. Hodder & Stoughton, London, 1985.

Walster, E., Aronson, V., Abrahams, D. & Rottman, L. "Importance of physical attractiveness in dating behaviour." *Journal of Personality and Social Psychology* 4 (1966), 508-16.

Westland, G. *Current Crises of Psychology*. Heinemann, London, 1978.

Weitz, S. (ed). *Nonverbal Communication*. Oxford University Press, 1974.

Wolf, N. *The Beauty Myth*. Vintage, 1990.

Index

A

accessories 52–3
adrenaline release 121
aesthetic intuition 60
androsterone 135
Argyle, Michael 68
arms 110–11
    crossed 111, 147, 148
    hand and arm signals 114–15
    wrists 114, 115, 147
arousal 8
attractiveness 154
auras 15
authentic attraction 13, 61
auto-erotic signalling 136, 137

B

back 118, 119
bars 8
belladonna 69
blinking 78, 79
blocking 39, 110
blonde hair 106
body hair 104
body talk 100–29
    arms 110–11
    back 118, 119
    buttocks 125
    chest and breasts 116–17
    dancing 122–3
    hair 104–5
    hands 112–15
    head, face and ears 102–4
    hips 124
    legs and feet 126–9
    neck 102, 106–7
    posture and movements 120–1
    shoulders 102, 108–9, 118
    stomach 118
the brain 11, 32
breasts 72, 73, 116, 117, 136
brunettes 105
buttocks 125

C

candlelit dinners 69
capulins 135
cars, flirting in traffic 30–1, 69
cell phone picture dating 133
chat rooms 133
cheek kissing 96
chests 116
city-dwellers, and personal space 19
closed-mouth smiles 86
clothes
    and accessories 52–3
    impressions made by 50–1
    invading personal space with 29
    and status 54

and touch 136
color
    of clothes 50
    colored contact lenses 67
    of hair 105
competence 10, 61
confidence 6
    self-confidence survey 55
    and sexual attraction 10, 11, 60
    and status 54–5
conflicting signals 148–9
conscious mind 8
contact lenses 67
courtship, early touch in 138–40
cowboy stance 112–13, 147
crossed arms 111, 147, 148
crossed legs 126, 148
    open 4 position 128
crotch display 128
crotch-pointing (cowboy stance)
    122–13, 147
cultural differences
    and hair 104
    and personal space 20–1
cultural influences 8
"cut-off" behavior 78

D

dancing 59, 122–3
dark hair 105
dating on-line 133
Davis, Bette 66
deception 150–1
designer labels 52
desire 8
diamond rings 52

E

e-mails 133
ears 103
eating 95
echoing 40, 44–5
environmental factors 37
evolutionary biology 11
expressive eyes 64–5
extroverts 17
eye contact 107
    eye-to-eye gazing 58, 64
    and handshakes 57
    inviting the gaze in 76–7
    peek-a-boo 38, 70, 80–1
    and personal space 18
    prolonged 70
    and sexual attraction 69
    in traffic 30, 69
eye make-up 66
eyebrows 75
    eyebrow flash 74, 80, 108, 112
    and smiling 88
eyelashes 79
eyes 62–81
    blinking 78, 79
    contact lenses 67

expressive 64–5
gazing 58, 64, 75, 76–7
glasses 67
large eyes 66
making the most of 66
pupil size 68
scanning the body 72–3
scanning the face 70–1
smiling 10, 67
staring 75
"wandering eye" syndrome 9, 37, 72
as windows of the soul 64
winking 78, 79
    two-eyed wink 79, 80

F

faces
    clasping face in hands 113
    facial expressions 33, 34–5
    scanning 70–1, 84
    and sexual attraction 102
    see also eyes; mouths
false smiles 86, 87, 88, 90
fans 80
feet
    "leaking" information 34, 35, 146
    playing footsie 129
    pointing with 36, 37
female proceptivity 11
first impressions 46–61
    attraction and aesthetics 60–1
    clothes 50–1
    handshakes 56–7
    listening to your feelings 59
    looking for visual clues 48–9
    making the first move 58–9
    power, confidence and status 54–5
food, playing with 138
full mirroring 41
full-face approaches, to invading
    personal space 26
full/broad smiles 87

G

gazing 58
    eye-to-eye 64, 75
    inviting the gaze in 76–7
glasses 67
global differences, and personal
    space 21
grooming, mutual 139

H

hair 104–5
half mirroring 41
hands 112–15
    accidentally touching 36
    caressing inanimate objects 114
    clasping face in 113
    early touch in courtship 138
    hand and arm signals 114–15
    holding 115
    invading personal space with 29,

114, 115
open-palm gestures 91, 114, 115, 146, 149
and deception 150, 152
pointing with 36, 37, 112, 113
wrists 114, 115
handshakes 29, 114
first impressions 56–7
two-hand shake 57
happiness 6, 61
heads
body talk with 102, 107
head tilt 146
hip-swinging 124
Hugo, Victor, *Les Miserables* 64
hunched shoulders 108

I J K
ice cream 84
Internet 132–3
intimate space 19
merging of 26–7
introverts 17
jewelry
neck jewelry 106, 116
rings 52
watches 52, 53
joy 6, 61
kissing 96–9

L
large eyes 66
laughter 6, 61, 89
leering 73
legs 124, 126–9
crossed 126, 148
open 4 position 128
parted 128
points 147
see also feet
lips
coloring 92, 93
enhancing 92–3
kissing 96–9
lip balm 89
pouting 85, 89
swollen 92
wet 92
listening skills 103
Lloyd-Elliott Rule of Four 144–7
lopsided shoulders 108
lopsided smiles 151
love at first sight 59
low self-esteem 54
lying 149, 150–3

M
make-up
eyes 66
lips 92, 93
making the first move 58–9
masked balls 80
men

and androsterone 135
arms 110, 111
buttocks 125
chests 116
competence in 10
conflicting signals 148, 149
core gender signals 49
cowboy stance 112–13, 147
and crotch display 128
and dancing 122
and driving 31
and face touching 102
and hair 104, 105
inviting the gaze in 76
making the first move 58–9
and necks 106
and personal space 20, 22, 23
and power play 19
rules for attracting women 9
scanning the body 72, 73
and sexual attraction 10, 11
and sexual desire 9
shoulders 108
stomachs 118
talking to women 103
and touching skills 138
"wandering eye" syndrome 9, 37, 72
and watches 53
winking 78, 79
menstrual cycle 7
mental health 7
mirroring 41–5, 146
body positions and space zones 42–3
full mirroring 41
half mirroring 41
putting into practice 44–5
Morris, Desmond 78
mouths 82–99
covering 84
enhancing the lips 92–3
kissing 96–9
and sexual arousal 94–5
sexy mouth and shape 84–5
smiling 34, 84, 86–91
touching 149, 150, 152
see also lips
mutual grooming 139

N O
necks 102, 106–7, 116, 117
non-verbal communication 7–13
non-verbal leakage 34
noses, touching 149, 152
"not interested" messages 8, 39, 40
objects
invading personal space with 28–9
leaving behind 29
passing 138
peek-a-boo using 80, 81
on-line dating 133
open body gestures 24–5

P
parties 138
peek-a-boo 38, 70, 80–1
perfumes 134, 135
personal space 16–31
and early touch in courtship 139
extroverts and introverts 17
intimate space 19, 26–7
invading 22–9
with hands 29, 114, 115
with objects 28–9
with open gestures and smiles 24–5
with our bodies 29
with pets 29
side-on and full-face approaches to 26–7
and power play 19
sex and cultural differences in 20–1
social space 19
and tactile tolerance 18
and territory 23
pets, invading personal space with 29
pheromones 134, 135
physical health 7
pointing 36–7, 102
crotch-pointing 122–13, 147
with feet 36, 37
with hands 36, 37, 112, 113
posture 120–1
pouting lips 85, 89
power
and handshakes 57
and status 54–5
power play 19
preening (self-touch) 136–7, 139, 146
hair 104, 105
proxemics 17, 20

R
red clothing 50
red hair 105
repulsion 8
rings 52
Rule of Four 144–7

S
scanning
bodies 72–3
faces 70–1, 84
scent 134–5
self-awareness 6
and mirroring 44
self-confidence see confidence
self-touch see preening (self-touch)
sexual attraction/arousal 8–13
and accessories 53
and aesthetics 60–1
and clothes 50–1
and dilated pupils 68
and eye contact 69
and the face 102
and female proceptivity 11

and hair 104
and handshakes 114
and kissing 96, 98
and mouths 85
and the neck 106–7
and the Rule of Four 144–7
and scents 135
and the senses 12–13
and sexual desire 9
and smiling 88–9
and teeth-baring 88
and visual clues 48–9
sexy mouths 84–5
shoes 52, 53
shoulders 102, 108–9, 118
side-on approaches, to invading
    personal space 26
signet rings 52
smell 134–5
smiling 34, 84, 86–91, 153
    closed-mouth smile 86
    and conflicting signals 148
    eyes 10, 67
    false smiles 86, 87, 88, 90
    full/broad smile 87
    genuine smiles 90–1
    lopsided 151
    and open gestures 24–5
    and pointing 112
    and teeth-baring 88
    and thoughts 88–9
    tight-lipped smile 86
social space 19

space zones, mirroring 42–3
staring 75
status
    and accessories 52, 53
    and handshakes 56, 57
    power and confidence 54–5
stomachs 118
swollen lips 92

T
T-shirt slogans 52
tactile tolerance 18
talking 154
teeth-baring 88
telephone calls 132, 133
territory, and personal space 23
thoughts, and smiling 88–9
tight-lipped smiles 86
torsos
    and dancing 122, 123
    sexy 118–19
touch 136–41
    early touch in courtship 138–40
    lovers 141
    see also preening (self-touch)
traffic, flirting in 30–1, 69
two-eyed wink 79, 80
two-hand shake 57

U V W
unconscious mind 8
visual clues, and first impressions 48–9
voice 132–3

"wandering eye" syndrome 9, 37, 72
watches 52, 53
wedding rings 52
wet lips 92
"white lies" 150
winking 78, 79
    two-eyed wink 79, 80
women
    backs 118, 119
    breasts 72, 73, 116, 117, 136
    buttocks 125
    and capulins 135
    conflicting signals 148
    core gender signals 49
    crotch display 128
    and dancing 122
    and face touching 102
    female proceptivity 11
    hair 104, 105
    inviting the gaze in 76
    and lip coloring 92, 93
    making the first move 58–9
    necks 106, 107
    and personal space 20, 22, 23
    and power play 19
    scanning the body 72, 73
    and sexual attraction 10, 11
    and sexual desire 9
    shoulders 108, 109, 118
    stomachs 118
    winking 79
work space, and personal space 23
wrists 114, 115, 147

Acknowledgments

Executive Editor Jane McIntosh
Editor Jessica Cowie
Executive Art Editor Karen Sawyer
Design Grade
Production Manager Ian Paton
Picture Research Aruna Mathur
Photographer Janeanne Gilchrist
Hair and make up Julie McGuire
Models Diane Wright, Ollie Benham,
Nana Wereko-Brobby, Will Beeslaar,
Christopher Muir, Laura Penny, Katy Kelly,
Duncan Forbes, Nicole Lewin, Charlie Belleville,
Marina Karapanovic

Picture credits
Corbis U.K. Ltd /Bettmann/Strauss/Curtis 16, 155;/
DiMaggio/Kalish 61;/Helen King 118;/Bill Miles 62.
Creatas/Stockbyte 51.
Getty Images 30, 31, 75, 77, 133.

Octopus Publishing Group Limited 24 right,
24 left, 65, 83, 98;/Janeanne Gilchrist 1–158;/
Colin Gotts 36, 38, 45 top, 45 bottom, 52 top,
74, 86 left, 86 right, 86 top, 87 bottom, 88 left,
88 right, 89 left, 89 right, 97, 99, 134–135;/
Peter Pugh-Cook 25 bottom right, 140 left,
140 right, 141.